50 Ways to Meet Your Lover

# 50 Ways
## to Meet Your Lover

~ *Following Cupid's Arrow* ~

Cathleen Rountree

HarperSanFrancisco
*A Division of* HarperCollins*Publishers*

HarperSanFrancisco and the author, in association with The Basic Foundation, a not-for-profit organization whose primary mission is reforestation, will facilitate the planting of two trees for every one tree used in the manufacture of this book.

A TREE CLAUSE BOOK

FIRST EDITION

Library of Congress Cataloging-in-Publication Data

Rountree, Cathleen.
   50 ways to meet your lover / Cathleen Rountree.
      p.   cm.
   ISBN 0–06–251188–2 (pbk. : alk. paper)
   1. Courtship.   2. Dating (Social customs).   3. Man-woman relationships.
I. Title.   II. Title: Fifty ways to meet your lover.
HQ801.R87   1995                                                      94–27620
646.7'7—dc20                                                          CIP
ISBN 0–06–251188–2

95  96  97  98  99  ❖  HAD  10  9  8  7  6  5  4  3  2  1

This edition is printed on acid-free paper that meets the American National Standards Institute Z39.48 Standard.

*To Ellen*

~

*To All Lovers:*

Those who have found each other
and those who are still looking

# Contents

# Foreword

This is a book about meetings. When the man or woman of our dreams becomes flesh and blood and is standing before us (or, in some cases, at the other end of a telephone), the reaction is immediate and palpable. There is an adrenaline rush that makes us ebullient, dazzled, euphoric. We have mad projections of a fulfilled future. We are devoured by desire and the impulse to be happy. The French call this initial meeting with a lover *coup de foudre;* they say we are "struck by lightning." Most of us have experienced this at least once.

In his classic novel, *Remembrance of Things Past*, the French writer Marcel Proust convincingly demonstrated that it takes many accidents, many surprising coincidences—and, perhaps, many efforts—to find the lover who, out of a thousand possibilities, suits our needs and desires.

The Jewish concept of *beshert* is humorously and poignantly illustrated in the movie *Sleepless in Seattle*. Why did so many of us love this film? Because we identified with the lovers; we *wanted* them to meet, fall in love, live happily ever after—because that is what we wish for ourselves. It reminded us of our own love story, or of the fact that we are still looking and hopeful. *Beshert* means one's destiny—the notion that when we are born, God chooses a life mate for us and that no matter where we live or what we do, we will eventually meet this person. We are *fated* to meet this person, and it becomes the disappointment of our lives if we don't. The good news is, even though we may have loved and lost in the past, there's always a second or third (or fourth or . . . ) crack at love. Cupid, with his vast experience and infinite wisdom, advises us that there are *countless* Mr. or Ms. Rights.

That first meeting between two people belongs to the world of coincidence and chance, synchronicity and serendipity, intuition and instinct, psychic maps and magic. It belongs to the world of Cupid, the Roman god of erotic love. What is it that makes you look twice at someone, find out her or his name, or ask him or her out to lunch? It's as if a window of opportunity opens up for one brief moment, and if it's not recognized and acted upon it is gone forever.

A few years after the death of my companion Sierra, a thirteen-year-old golden retriever, I decided to find a new ally. I'd been gripped by an advertisement for the SPCA and thought I'd try my luck there. On my third visit I found an English springer spaniel I named Sienna. He was my canine counterpart: expressive brown eyes, long hair—auburn and naturally wavy—and abundant energy. He became my new best friend. It had been so simple. Why couldn't there be an SPCL, I wondered—a Society for the Prevention of Cruelty to Lovers. I imagined row after row of charming bungalows filled with women and men of all ages, sizes, professions, backgrounds, and appearances. They were up-to-date on their shots, had been thoroughly screened for health problems, and had good teeth; their former partners had written extensive evaluations; there were character and financial profiles available (maybe even a video); and some, by their own request, had been neutered.

I found the idea entertaining and *very* practical: whenever a relationship ended, I'd be off to the local branch of the SPCL, where I'd systematically and *pragmatically* find a new partner rather than allowing my hormones to make these important choices for me.

But life isn't so logical or convenient. It holds many mysterious and magical meanderings for us. This is a book for those of us who are still looking for that special person—the significant other, the soul mate, the man or woman of our dreams. As these fifty stories will reassure you, he or she not only is out there, but is looking for *you*, too, and you will probably find her or him when you least expect it. *Bonne chance!*

*Cathleen Rountree*
*Aptos, California*
*July 1994*

# ~ 1 ~

# Single White Female

For Eleanor, finding the right man was no easy task. She was divorced and had had several disappointing love affairs. Maybe the personals *would* work for her, she thought, even though friends had cautioned her against trying them.

"I am traditional, yet unconventional," her announcement read, "and I am looking for a nondrinking, available man of power." Eleanor had spent a month writing and rewriting the ad. Within a week she had received nearly thirty responses at her safely anonymous post-office box. Reading the letters carefully, she chose five of the most interesting and suitable and called her admirers.

She says she knew it was "him" during their first telephone conversation: "There was no holding back. None of the fearful, noncommittal crap I'd experienced so often in men. He was so open and honest and present."

Bill says he knew it was "her" the first time they met: "In Eleanor's company I felt like I'd finally come home. I knew I'd met the woman I wanted to marry."

The fact that they not only appreciated each other's physical attributes but also shared a value system and life goals assured them that they were right for one another. They have now been married for twelve years and swear they owe it all to the personals.

&❧ Cupid says:

Finding the right person is often a process of elimination. There are countless Mr. and Ms. Rights out there. Be as clear as you can in your own mind and heart about the qualities you are seeking in a mate. This takes self-knowledge. What are the qualities in a partner that you couldn't live without: honesty, intelligence, fidelity, a sense of humor? Whatever they are, don't waver from these core principles. There are plenty of occasions for compromise and adjustment on less important matters.

# ~ 2 ~

# Novocaine or Laughing Gas?

In 1974 Elizabeth moved to Napa, California, but she missed the hustle and bustle of her former life in Berkeley. Two years after her move, while spending a weekend with her family and close friends in the East Bay, she found herself responding with pleasure to the familiar sights of downtown Berkeley on a lovely summer day. From one of the dozen or so purveyors of street food she bought a soft pretzel. As she bit into it, she learned that you have to be careful of oxymorons: yelping "Ouch," she discovered she'd broken one of her molars in half. It didn't bother her afterward, but she thought she'd better have it checked out anyway, just in case.

It didn't seem to her it had been *that* long since she'd last visited her dentist, but it must have been, because she discovered he was now retired. Finally, Elizabeth found a dentist who observed Friday banking hours: he stayed open until six o'clock.

Everyone liked Ernie. He was funny and easygoing, and he made each of his patients feel special, like he really cared about *them*. Elizabeth had an inexplicable queasy feeling when she first saw Ernie. She found herself immensely attracted to him.

"I swear it was love at first sight," Ernie says today about their first meeting. "The moment she walked into my office, my heart opened to her."

"I met someone this afternoon I think is really wonderful," Elizabeth told her friends that evening. They laughed when she said that the someone was her dentist. Out of curiosity she looked up his home address in the phone book. When she saw him listed in a single-family neighborhood, she assumed he was married. It had been a long time since she'd been so attracted to someone, and she'd learned to accept and enjoy her life as a single woman, and to really appreciate her large circle of friends. She was so happy just to have been attracted to a man once more that it didn't much matter to her if she saw him again.

When she went back for her crown in November, Elizabeth discovered, much to her surprise, that Ernie was also interested in her. He invited her to picnic with him in Redwood Park. After that there was a period of tentative dancing at local clubs, phone calls, and visits during which they began to build their friendship and pursue their romantic affection.

In order to get her attention, he sent her flowers at work and made a special effort to make friends with those of Elizabeth's friends who were skeptical of him. But Ernie made his biggest impression on Elizabeth when, after she casually mentioned that she wanted to learn to play the piano, he had one delivered to her house. "It took up half the living space," she laughs, remembering his impressive gift.

Eventually she moved back to the East Bay and they began living together. After eighteen years of cohabitation and two children, Elizabeth says, "It was pretty romantic. Still is!"

ह॰ Cupid says:

There is nothing like thoughtful consideration to get someone's attention. A gift is always an appropriate way to show that you care. It's not the size of the gift that counts; it's the unexpected quality, the awareness of what would really be special and meaningful, what would really please the person. And you can discover that only by listening and observing carefully.

~ 3 ~

# The Latin Connection

When Norma left her all-girls Catholic high school and started at the Jesuit college in Cleveland, she quickly learned two things: that she was attractive to men; and that she loved being in an environment in which the ratio of men to women was three to one. What choices! Life was just beginning.

It was the first week of her second year. Although Norma had loads of men as friends, she'd never had an official date. This seemed odd to her peers, but in her Puerto Rican family this strict code of behavior was not only encouraged but enforced. In her relationships with both men and women the question inevitably arose of why she had to be home by five o'clock on weekday afternoons and by ten on weekends. Although she was born in the United States, she spent summers with her extended family in Puerto Rico, and she liked the fact that her family spoke only Spanish at home in

Cleveland. Her Latin heritage was a strong part of her identity, and she savored it.

Norma and her friend Nicky were sitting on the front steps of the college chapel after Mass, the fragrant smoke of frankincense drifting from the sanctuary. As Nicky's friend Mauricio approached them, Norma was at once both soothed and made dizzy by his handsome face and athletic body. She had trouble breathing as he stretched out his hand toward her.

"*De donde eres?*" he asked.

Hardly believing her ears, Norma responded with a slight blush, "*Soy puerto riqueña.*"

"I'm from Chile," Mauricio smiled, filling in the gap that her stunned silence had created. After some small talk with Nicky, Mauricio said, "Next week is Chile's independence day. Why don't you two come with me to the soccer game?"

As Norma watched Mauricio play soccer with trim agility, she realized how glad she was to have met him and how much they shared just by both being Latin. After the game ended, he ran to the sidelines and asked for Norma's telephone number.

When he called her later that evening, she felt relieved to be able to talk with someone who understood her parents' strict parameters for her (his parents had similar rules for his sister, who was Norma's age) and was willing to work within them, who accepted and *appreciated* that her family spoke Spanish at home (his did so, too), who knew the pleasures of eating rice and beans. He would pick her up on Friday night at seven.

Friday night was a milestone for Norma *and* her parents: it was her first unchaperoned date. As she had anticipated, Mauricio was completely comfortable with the ritual required to get her out of the house. It began with a shot of Puerto Rican rum and continued with a bit of semi-investigative questioning by Norma's parents.

"*Si!* We left in 1973," explained Mauricio, placing himself in the politically correct segment of Chileans who fled just before and after the coup and Salvador Allende's assassination. "My father is a cardiologist, and I plan to become a doctor as well. . . . I understand; I will have Norma back by eleven."

Instead of attending the campus dance that night, which had originally been their plan, they sat on a park bench in the inner city, not far from Norma's home, and, in the stew and humidity of a Midwestern September, did what most hot-blooded teenagers do. Her parents would have been aghast!

Now married and looking back twenty years, Norma and Mauricio believe that if they had met in Chile, they probably wouldn't have dated. "My blue-collar background would have been out of his class," explains Norma. "I would have been a poor Puerto Rican girl dating a wealthy Latin American. We love our countries of origin, but feel very lucky to have met in America."

## ᑫ Cupid says:

Cultural similarities can provide an automatic basis for interaction and understanding between two people. Although in other countries class distinctions may be stronger deterrents for couples, they are, unfortunately, all too real in the United States as well. Sometimes you have to outsmart your rational mind, which thinks it knows everything. You each must overcome your prejudices again and again until you train yourselves out of them.

The emotional comfort and physical pleasure you feel with a particular person can't be manufactured; they either exist or they don't—no matter what your mind says is best for you. People may choose a partner for many different reasons, but the bottom line is: if you are unable to be completely yourself with that person, forget it!

# A House of One's Own

Janet was a victim of early burnout syndrome in her mid-thirties. She was a single mother, and as the owner of a television research company, she was getting tired of the career ladder. The idea of ditching it all, doing the back-to-nature trip, appealed to her enormously.

She certainly didn't plan on falling head over heels for Blair, the instructor of the Build Your Own Home course she took that summer. Besides, he was married. "I was enough of a feminist to know I didn't want another woman's husband," she remembers. But a caring friendship nonetheless developed between them.

When Blair offered Janet the chance of an indefinite stay at his log cabin in the Berkshires as a retreat, she jumped at the opportunity for solitude. "I stayed on the mountain for two years, driving into town once a week," she recalls. "I had given up on the possibility of ever meeting a man and marrying again. And it was okay."

They had at first thought that theirs was meant to be a working relationship only, rather than one as life partners. But their friendship deepened over time, and after spending a long weekend with each other they decided to throw their lots together.

It had taken them four years to make the decision to sever their individual ties and embark on a new beginning. They were both forty. Since then they have written several successful books together. "We've had to work really hard at making a go of it," says Janet. "After the first six months, we fought for a full year. It was all about power. I had to learn that Blair was not going to solve my life's problems. We have a deep relationship; it changes and evolves. After ten years it still gets better and better."

### ❧ Cupid says:

You don't have to live in a city and go to parties every night in order to meet someone. Sometimes it takes being alone for a while to really know what you are looking for in a relationship. The most important consideration is to nourish yourself, and that often means a period of solitude. Instead of fearing time alone, welcome it. Friends had told Janet, "You'll never meet a man if you're living out in the woods in a log cabin." Yet her priority was not to meet a man but to nurture her soul. She ended up doing both.

## ~ 5 ~

# Making Movies

Marilyn was down to counting her pennies. She didn't know how she would pay the next month's rent. Although she had sworn off secretarial work, a concerned friend had set up an interview for her with a well-known Hollywood director who was looking for an assistant. She entered the room, she says, "shaking like a leaf"—not because she wanted the job so desperately, but because she so desperately *didn't* want the job. "I didn't even know why I was there. As I came through the door I went into a complete anxiety state and began to stutter—which I'd never done before in my life."

Andrew seemed like an amiable man, and to put her at ease he asked her a question about her father, also a successful film director. "You want to talk about my f-f-f-father," she stammered, withdrawing further into herself at the thought that he was more interested in her father than in her. Seeing her nervousness, but not wishing to end the interview, Andrew calmly suggested, "Why don't we just relax, have a cigarette, and not talk about anything for a couple of minutes?"

When Marilyn had calmed down sufficiently, he asked her why she wanted the job. "The truth is, I don't," she replied. "I really just want to write, but I need to pay my rent. I love movies, and I heard you were a really nice guy."

Appreciating her candor, he then described the job to her, explaining that he thought of the relationship between director and assistant as "a kind of marriage."

"Marriage!" she gasped. "I don't even know how to spell the word!"

She got the job. Why? "She had the same ambivalence I did about career goals, about the industry, about work in general," Andrew explains. "We'd interviewed plenty of people who type faster, but something told me she'd be a lot more fun to have around."

As they began working together she proved to be an invaluable asset, and their mutual affection began to grow. A year later they were shooting a film on location in the Caribbean, and in that beautiful tropical setting their friendship turned to romance, true love, and, eventually, marriage.

ॐ Cupid says:

It pays to be yourself. Eventually your true self and motivation emerge anyway, so why waste time? There are many "experts" and know-it-alls around, but few people are willing to openly reveal their insecurities, their lack of a complete mastery of life. Vulnerability is often a person's most attractive quality—in work *or* love.

## ~ 6 ~

# Cyberspace Romance

The antithetical proverbs "Seeing is believing" and "Looks can be deceiving" both have their basis in truth; and either one can be used to justify or support a particular view of an encounter between two people, assuming the encounter is face-to-face. But cyberspace, E-mail, on-line, techno-talk, or typeface-to-typeface—as the medium of electronic communications is variously called—brings with it a need for a new method of discerning character, personality, and, when you get right down to it, *reality*.

A computer screen full of words, as Linda learned from personal experience, can provide a safe medium for getting to know someone without the usual barriers of prejudice based on appearance. But beware cyber-cads! Because the nuances of facial expression, body language, and tone of voice (all of which people subliminally rely upon to form judgments of others even more than they do the actual words they may hear) are missing, an on-line persona can be used to purposely mislead, hustle, and hoodwink others.

"I met 'Mr. X' on-line," Linda recounts. "He seriously romanced me via E-mail." Their involvement soon upgraded to the telephone, and within a few weeks they met in person. "I could tell he wasn't the man of my dreams when we met, but I wanted to continue our on-line communiqués." Through a fluke during the week following their meeting, however, Linda accidentally discovered that Mr. X had been concurrently cyber-seducing several other women! A minor scandal ensued, and an emotionally bruised but wiser Linda emerged, ready to meet a new man.

≈ ≈ ≈

"I wasn't looking for a romantic involvement," says Michael, "but I kept running into Linda at on-line community parties." There wasn't any spark between them at first, but they had a chance to get to know each other by reading what the other had written on-line.

"In person, Michael did not appear to be the type of man in whom I would have been interested," Linda reports. "But on-line I had the opportunity to see how his mind works, how bright he is, and how thoughtfully he communicates. My initial resistance was overcome by how deliciously he communicates with the written word." She found it refreshing to interact with someone in a medium that eliminates some common forms of prejudice.

Within a short time Linda and Michael's on-line communication became more intimate. One night after a party they found themselves going out to dinner together. Sitting quietly alone with each other for the first time, they both felt a connection "so real that we looked around for the little fat guy with the arrow," laughs Michael. "Cupid must have had something to do with it."

## ᙠ Cupid says:

People nowadays seldom use writing as a means of getting to know one another. Yet when they do so, dimensions of a person that might otherwise be filtered out are allowed to emerge. Electronic communications can be a safe and satisfying place to meet and interact with people, and a genuine sense of community can be found or developed.

However, someone with a vivid imagination can easily become deeply invested in an illusion of another person. It's best to temper cyberspace romance with a large dose of reality. Whether or not you actually launch a computer-based courtship after an on-line introduction, you will have entered a fascinating world of communication ranging in subjects from arts and entertainment to social responsibility and politics. Log on today!

# Caught in the Elevator

"Who would believe we met in an elevator in Hollywood?" asks Carol.

Mel had felt an instant pang when he saw her. "She was cute, but it wasn't just looks. There was something about her energy that interested me. I don't know, maybe Cupid shot an arrow into my heart," he laughs.

You don't have much time to act in an elevator, so he quickly invited her out to lunch. Definitely not a demure woman, Carol apologized, saying she was late for a meeting. Yet something in her had responded to his ability and willingness to think and act fast.

That could have been that. But outside, as he got into his car, Mel looked around and saw a grinning Carol in her car, pulled up alongside him. "I can't go to lunch now, but where would we go if we were going?"

Taking the bait, Mel mentioned a well-known eatery down the street on Sunset Boulevard. "Well, maybe I could go for dinner," she proposed. That night they met at Chin Chin and have been together ever since.

ॐ Cupid says:

An opportunity with a particular person may come only once. When you feel that recognizable pang in your heart, take action! Opportunities come and go like a breeze on a windy day.

# Love Is (a) Blind (Date)

*It'll be a double date, so I won't be alone with this guy*, she thought. They'd have a congenial dinner with her friends, and two weeks later Maurine would be back in London to receive her divorce settlement, which would allow her an unfettered period of time to devote to her writing. She'd grown to love London: the dependable morning fog; fish and chips served bundled in the *Times;* the quaint, crammed-to-the-hilt bookshops that served tea; even wintertime's bitter cold. But it was enjoyable being back in L.A., too, especially during the summer.

That morning had felt like a turning point in her life. Because of a persistent pain in her left fibula, for the past week she had endured endless testing and X rays to determine whether she had bone cancer. Sitting in a white hospital gown, the kind that doesn't close in the back, she was exhilarated to feel the cold stainless-steel gurney against her buttocks as the doctor said, "We can't find any-thing wrong with you."

It seemed like a miracle, a second chance, to her as she sat on the curb outside the doctor's office bursting with a confusing residue of terror and newly gained relief. "I will go to Africa and take care of sick children, God—whatever you want me to do," Maurine promised with the gratitude and innocence of a child. "My life is yours!" She would wait for a word from God.

≈ ≈ ≈

Peter was short, with the athletic build of a martial-arts champion—which, indeed, he was. Definitely a man who could take care of himself and anyone else put under his charge. In his late thirties, di-vorced, and sharing the custody of his four-year-old daughter, he had systematically drawn up a list of the qualities he wanted in a woman. That weekend alone, he had four dates scheduled. Maurine was number two.

It was her first taste of sushi, and she had the sense that she'd never be bored with this man, that there would always be new expe-riences with him. They didn't touch or kiss, but talked as if they'd known each other for a very long time. They shared the unspoken feeling that they somehow fit. In his mind, he canceled dates three and four.

When she arrived back at her parents' home that night, where she was staying, Maurine said, "I know this sounds crazy, but I think I just met the man I'm going to marry." Since she was still legally married, her parents looked at each other and thought, *Good grief! What next?*

The next morning Maurine was called to the phone. "Will you see me tonight?" asked Peter's hopeful voice on the other end. Monday, two days later, was the soonest she was free. It would have to do.

Sunday, two dozen yellow roses arrived at her parents' house. Monday, there were long-stemmed red roses. Peter was "sweeping" and Maurine was falling. That night during a romantic candlelit dinner, Peter told her, "You are the purest gold I've ever met. I'd be a fool to let you go. What shall we do?" Thinking at first that he was propositioning her for an affair, she was bewildered when he went on to ask her to marry him. They spent the following two hours discussing what they each wanted from life and imagining what a life together would be like. Was this the sign she was looking for?

Was Maurine certain this was what *she* wanted? It had all happened so fast. Was the message from God "a new husband and children"? *What about me?* pleaded her creative side. *You've now got the money, time, and solitude to write.* What should she do? Peter was used to making offers that couldn't be refused. She'd never been wanted so badly by anyone.

Six months later, on December 25, they eloped to Lake Tahoe and were married by the Reverend Michael Love. "I was his final tax deduction of the year," laughs Maurine.

Two hundred seventy-two days later, when she gave birth to their first child, David, the Word became flesh.

## ঔ Cupid says:

When you don't trust yourself to make the correct and practical decisions concerning your life, it seems easier, safer, to put the burden of responsibility on something out- side yourself. It's true there are invisible forces at work that are beyond your control. The world works through you and you work through the world in mysterious ways; there is a continual interchange. Signs, messages, and omens concerning both sides of a question can be found every- where. Be still within yourself, listen to your intuition and instincts, make your decision, and do your best to follow through. Human beings are always looking for an absolute. There is no absolute, but there *are* hope and hard work and luck.

# Nature Lovers

Nature and the outdoors were Jessica's passion. She was happiest skiing, kayaking, riding her mountain bike, and, especially, river rafting. Since high school she had spent her spring and summer vacations as a river guide. Soon she would be graduating from the University of Colorado, where she'd been for four years. But first she would enjoy two weeks of riding the rapids on the Salmon River during spring break.

Jessica's skill as a river guide had landed her a position at a river-guide school for those two weeks. Teaching other guides allowed her to share her years of experience in close calls, her anecdotes of first-time rafters, and her favorite campsite recipes.

She and her friend Mandy camped along the edge of the river their first night. Instruction would begin the next day. She'd already noticed the telemark skis and the mountain bike atop a Range Rover in the parking lot, but she hadn't yet seen the owner.

Tom had taken a leisurely drive up from Santa Fe to Idaho, and he looked forward to the opportunity the guide school offered him to be on the river and learn a new skill that would help him make the wilderness more accessible to other nature lovers. The training was only one week long, but he would learn a lot and enjoy his time.

*He looks interesting,* Jessica thought to herself when she saw Tom unloading his backpack from the athletically equipped automobile. Not knowing exactly how to approach him, she didn't. But she was relieved and excited to see Tom among the group of new trainees. There would be six people in Jessica's boat—and boy was she glad that the man from the parking lot was one of them! There was a mutual attraction between the two, and the elements of nature contributed a romantic backdrop that added to their enjoyment. After a week together they each knew they'd found in the other a solid friend and fellow outdoor adventurer.

### ᖍ᙭ Cupid says:

For nature lovers there is nothing better than finding someone with whom to share their first love. Obviously, the place to find these people is through activities in nature. Hiking, trekking, rafting, camping, kayaking, mountain biking, scuba diving, swimming, skiing, roller blading, sailing—all have their devotees. Join a local sports club or group. Attend lectures and slide presentations about nature excursions. Check out your city's mycological or wildflower society and go along for the "hunt."

# Harlem Renaissance

They met in Harlem, where they both lived during the Great Depression. It was a vital time in Harlem—just after the black renaissance. The Roosevelt administration had recently established the Works Progress Administration program, which provided work to artists of all kinds: painters, dancers, musicians, writers, playwrights, and poets. "In retrospect," says the renowned African American artist Jacob Lawrence, "you realize what a wonderful program the WPA was, even though the country was going through a terrible economic trauma."

In 1935 there were two WPA centers in Harlem, which enabled young people like Jacob to receive instruction and direction in whatever art form interested them. "It didn't mean that we would necessarily become professional artists. We didn't think of it that way at the time. But it was a place we could explore music, theater, literature, dance, and painting." The centers were also likely meeting places and safe hangouts for the community's youth. Even people from outside the Harlem community took an interest and would visit the centers.

Gwen Knight had been born in Barbados and had moved to Harlem with her family when she was thirteen. At twenty, Gwen, a fun-loving and ethereally beautiful young woman, became a regular student and model at sculptress Augusta Savage's studio, which was part of one of the WPA centers. Gwen had attended Howard University for her first two years of college, where she majored in painting, but because of economic hardship her parents had no longer been able to afford to support her education. She gladly took advantage of the Art Center. There she met and became friends with the slightly younger Jacob.

Those who attended the center's offerings of classes and exhibitions formed a group and together would visit museums and galleries throughout the city. The center sponsored frequent lectures, and many interesting people would talk about their respective craft and its challenges. "It was part of our learning experience—a wonderful period," recalls Gwen.

Jacob and Gwen had common interests. Each was curious about the other's artwork. So when did romance color the picture? "These things happen," laughs Jacob, "but you don't realize it at the time. First, you know you enjoy the company of the other person. Then you find out you're compatible . . ."

". . . and then you get married," Gwen adds with a smile. "In *those* days you got married. These days couples just live together and maybe they'll get married, maybe not."

"We didn't have to declare our love immediately," says Jacob. "These things grow, they develop. Many of our friends had similar experiences." They admit that relationships seemed more relaxed then. People were more interested in making long-term friends than in finding a husband or wife.

Gwen feels that couples are swept away by the romantic notion of love—the idea that you must fall in love and then can't live without that other person. But, she points out, artists are not involved in "majority" thinking: "They have a different perspective on how they live their lives." Because their work is the focus of their attention, Gwen believes, artists are more willing and able to see romance as a fairy tale. As an example of this view, she recounts the following story:

"Shortly after we were married in 1938, we took a trip to New Orleans. Friends said, 'Oh, you're going on your honeymoon!' It had never entered our minds that we were having a honeymoon. We went to meet new people, experience a new culture. As an artist you are interested in people for who they are. You relate to someone who is doing the same things you're doing, thinking the same things you're thinking. And maybe love grows, slowly."

## 🦢 Cupid says:

Having similar backgrounds, environments, ancestry, and cultures and sharing common thoughts, feelings, imaginings, and dreams can bring natural compatibility to a relationship, romantic or otherwise. You don't have to be an artist to recognize the validity of Gwen and Jacob's words: "Couples are swept away by the romantic notion of love." Involve yourself in group activities and focus more on creating long-term friendships than on finding a husband or a wife. Go to the places your interests lead you and you will find like-minded and -hearted friends.

# No Wedding Bell Blues

For Janmarie and Marius it was a classic case of love at first sight. "Our eyes met across a crowded room," Marius reminisces. The crowded room happened to be the hall where the wedding reception of a mutual friend was taking place.

Janmarie says she felt like someone had slapped her. While trying to maintain a cool facade, she was "flipping out inside." The moment was so unnerving for them both that they stayed as far away from each other as possible until the end of the party, when she approached him, cautiously.

"I knew something that only happens once in a lifetime to a woman was happening to me right now, and I had to take a closer look," Janmarie remembers. She didn't know whether Marius had been equally affected, but she went ahead and opened the conversation by self-consciously saying, "It's funny; we seem to know all the same people."

After a few minutes of talking with Marius, Janmarie noticed an eyelash in his irritated eye and offered to remove it. Then while he stood rubbing his newly relieved eye, she disappeared into the ladies' room. "My heart was throbbing, I couldn't take the intensity," Janmarie says.

Half expecting Marius to be gone when she emerged, she instead found him waiting for her near the exit. As he walked her to her car, he calmly seemed to read her thoughts as he began, "Something happened this afternoon . . ." She invited him out for dinner that night. They hardly ate, but rather stared into each other's eyes, trying to understand the magic that had touched them. Both felt there was an unbreakable bond between them and that they'd found each other.

Two years later Marius and Janmarie are living together and working out the practicalities of sharing life as a couple.

## ࢣ Cupid says:

> Beware. Weddings are Cupid's favorite event. Everyone should have at least one love-at-first-sight experience. Even though your mind might be saying, "Watch out! This can't possibly work," it doesn't hurt to check things out. This particular person may not be your life mate, but you might nevertheless learn a valuable lesson from the person about yourself, love, or life. And you might have some fun in the process.

# Enchanted in Bali

Judy had been traveling to Bali for five consecutive years, leading art and cultural study tours, and was interested in researching and writing a book about Balinese masks and culture. One sunny afternoon, she and an American girlfriend were sitting on the porch of the house where she was staying, which overlooked verdant terraced rice fields. A local acquaintance stopped by with a friend, who was introduced as Surya. Surya didn't speak English.

Judy's Scandinavian features, long blond hair, and fair skin were a striking counterpoint to Surya's exotic Indonesian dark good looks. During a lull in the conversation, while the acquaintance went to get ice for their drinks (leaving Surya in the care of the two women), Judy turned to her American friend and said, "He's really good looking, isn't he?"

"Yes, he's got beautiful eyes."

"And a great mouth!"

A few days later, Judy, alone this time, walked into a crowded local gathering place, the Nomad. Without realizing it she sat next to Surya, who began speaking rapidly to her in Indonesian. "Slowly, slowly," she said, reminding him of her faltering Indonesian.

"Okay, we'll practice English," he replied in *perfect* English. She was mortified after realizing he had surely understood her earlier ravings about his beauty.

That evening they fumbled through a half-English, half-Indonesian conversation about Balinese art, culture, and politics, which struck her as unusual, because the Balinese are fearful of speaking their minds, living in a military dictatorship as they do. She found him thoughtful, intelligent, articulate, and of course beautiful.

They spent the remainder of Judy's trip together but didn't see each other again until her next tour a year later, when they picked up where they had left off. Over the next few years an unlikely relationship developed between them, and they were married six years ago. They now lead tours together and divide their time between California and Bali.

## ॐ Cupid says:

> Traveling in foreign countries can make people more open and responsive to new romantic experiences. There are many fascinating guided tours available to satisfy every intellectual, artist, seeker, collector, gourmet, or sports enthusiast: archaeology in the Yucatán, textiles in Guatemala,

watercolor painting in Greece, hiking in Wales, temples and stone gardens in Kyoto, wine tours in France, meditation in India, snorkeling in Australia, cross-country skiing in Norway. Major universities offer guided tours, as does the Smithsonian Institution, and there are numerous reputable touring companies. Send away for their free catalogues and enjoy the process of researching where you want to go. If you are wary of traveling alone, find a good friend who is enthusiastic about travel to go with you.

## ~ 13 ~

# Is There a Doctor in the House?

San Francisco was on the verge of the Summer of Love in 1965. Linda, a doctor of anesthesiology, was on the staff at Children's Hospital. She and her friend Shirley were sitting in the operating-room office one afternoon prior to an upcoming surgery when a tall, well-built, fair-haired man entered the room. As the women sat gossiping about the hospital staff, the man walked over to a row of shelves in front of them and stretched up to fetch something from the top shelf. Shirley poked Linda in the arm and nodded her head toward the extended figure. "Look at that body. Look at those buns!" she exclaimed in a hushed tone.

With a little investigation Linda learned that the man was an orthopedic surgeon who had been sent to Children's Hospital for his last year of training. She continued to keep an inquisitive eye on him and to hang out where she would most likely encounter him.

"I see you're curious about astrology," the man, whose name was Jerry, said to Linda one night. Strewn across the table was a ream of papers covered with astrological charts for her friends. Because of her scientific orientation, precision was very important to Linda. In order to find the accurate longitudes and latitudes for the charts, she used logarithms. However, mathematics had never been her strong suit, and Jerry, who had begun to take an interest in her interest, decided to assist her with the math.

"What's your sign?" she was soon asking him. "I find I'm attracted to men who have Scorpio on their ascendant. It makes them dark and sexy," she added alluringly.

*Bingo!* he thought to himself. He went home and diligently began researching his own chart. He'd never put much stock in astrology, but he now saw it as a useful tool.

"This is incredible," Jerry told Linda the next day. "I have Scorpio rising." Of course he didn't tell her that he'd fudged the hour of his birth to move it up a few degrees from Libra. They continued to run into each other during and after surgeries, ostensibly to discuss the finer calibrations of astrology.

One night Linda was on second call at home (meaning she was available for backup if there was an overflow of emergencies). Her friend Russell called: "You'd better get in here pronto. There's a major emergency." It was midnight and she'd been reading in bed, but she had her hospital clothes at hand. Not bothering to comb her hair or apply any makeup, out the door she tore.

She was breathless when she arrived in the emergency room. Oddly, she found no other staff members—only a covered figure lying on a gurney. As she approached it she saw that it was Jerry lying there in wait, a huge grin on his face. It had been a setup, but a clever one—and successful.

Two years later, their wedding invitations announced the horoscope of their wedding day, and their wedding cake was decorated with the same horoscope. It was November 16—the sign of Scorpio—a dark and sexy day.

### ࿔ Cupid says:

Asking "What's your sign?" is a harmless way to introduce yourself to someone. Not only is playing the horoscope game fun, but it can be productive. Those who follow the guidelines of astrology can learn much about themselves and a potential lover. Just out of curiosity, discover which astrological signs are best suited to your sun, moon, and rising signs. How compatible were you with past loves in your life? What were their signs? Is there any accuracy in the astrological information on you and them?

# My Mother, the Matchmaker

That night, Ruth wore a royal blue full-length formal to her cousin's wedding. It made her look several years older than her youthful fifteen. As she walked, the taffeta petticoats underneath made the dress seem like it was moving silently along on a conveyor belt, the body inside just a prop. The year was 1936, and *Gone with the Wind* had been published only the month before. Before her family left home for the wedding, Ruth had felt like Scarlett O'Hara on her way to attend a ball in Atlanta—glamorous and grown-up—even though the country was in the midst of the Great Depression and she was terribly shy. By the time she reached the hall where the ceremony was to take place, Ruth's shyness overcame her.

"I'm not going in. I'm not!" she declared.

"Get out of that car," her father thundered at her.

Always the appeaser, Clara, Ruth's mother, coddled and humored her daughter. "I promise you you'll have a good time. I guarantee it!" she swore.

As her only other option was to spend several hours in the car alone, Ruth acceded. It was to be one of those large gatherings at which you see every member of your family and then some. It might not be so bad.

Waiting for the ceremony to begin, she stood in a corner alone while her parents mingled, and watched the activity flutter around her. When she looked up to an overhanging balcony she saw two good-looking young men. They seemed also to have noticed Ruth as they talked back and forth to each other, giggling behind their hands. *So, the evening has promise*, she thought.

After the words "You may kiss the bride" had been spoken and the orchestra had struck up "Love Is Here to Stay," people began filing into the dining room for dinner. The two men from the balcony were now lingering in the archway Ruth had to pass through on her way to the dining room. Suddenly, she felt a familiar hand on her arm and heard her mother say to them, "Hello. What's your name? This is my daughter, Ruth." The tune "I Only Have Eyes for You" seemed to pour out of one of the young men's eyes as he stared at Ruth. His name was Leo, and, as it turned out, his family was on friendly terms with Clara's.

"He's a good boy. He comes from a fine family," Clara later told her confidently when Ruth mentioned that Leo had invited her out on a date.

The next weekend, only hours before he was to pick her up, Leo called to say he was at the hospital because his brother had broken his leg but that they would go out the next week. "Sure!" Ruth steamed. By the following weekend, she'd forgotten which man was which and was expecting not Leo but his friend, Hal. When Leo popped up she was surprised, but not for long.

The couple became an established item—much to Clara's chagrin. *What have I done?* she asked herself as she fretted, trying to convince Ruth that she was too young to go steady and should really play the field.

Less than three years later they were married on a shoestring in the home of Ruth's parents. For fifty-three years they maintained a devotion to each other that had first glimmered in Leo's eyes when he saw the beautiful young girl in the royal blue satin gown.

ॐ Cupid says:

It doesn't matter how old you may be—fifteen or sixty-five. When you meet the mate that fate created you for, you'll know it. Behold kismet!

## ~ 15 ~

# The Professor and the Spy Who Loved Him

Their predicament was like something out of a movie—a grade-B movie—because who could believe it?

Ten months before the massacre of demonstrating students at Tiananmen Square, a middle-aged American history professor from San Jose State University named Larry was teaching at the Center for Chinese and American Studies in Nanjing. He was part of an academic exchange program sponsored by Johns Hopkins University.

Writing a book on the fall of Saigon, he was in steady correspondence with top Vietnamese military officials. Beijing became suspicious of the unmindful professor, and he became a watched man.

~ ~ ~

Xu Meihong was a beautiful young woman, one of fifty enrolled in Larry's course on American history and culture. She was also a first lieutenant of the Institute for International Relations of the People's Liberation Army; in other words, she was a spy.

To him she was at first simply another student, another difficult name to pronounce on the roster. But one day they walked to the post office together. A raconteur by nature, Larry entertained her with his whimsical accounts of the lives of passers-by. When he asked her to join in, she became mute. His was a game of the imagination, and she had no idea how to play.

Their first date as friends consisted of a Western meal at the Jinling Hotel—a hamburger ("A lousy one, at that," Larry remembers). Within a few weeks they knew they were in love.

Meihong had already been assigned to watch for someone in the CIA teaching at the center. Larry became suspicious of Meihong's inordinate interest in his political leanings and her probings into his personal life: "She knew my daughters' names, and she'd been reading my mail before it even got to me. One day, she asked why I'd had such a huge bill—three thousand dollars—on my Macy's account. I flipped." He angrily began his own line of questioning.

Within minutes Meihong, amid tears, was revealing a fantastic story of espionage and intrigue. She admitted that his phone was tapped and his mail routinely opened. "Why me?" he asked with disbelief. "Because they think you are an American agent" was Meihong's logical reply.

Meihong was arrested and told she had betrayed the military by exposing her government to a dangerous American spy. She endured interminable interrogations, beatings, cold, and filth. Her interrogators told her that Larry was a threat to her country, a playboy who wasn't serious about her. But one day she had an epiphany: she realized that even if all that his detractors said about him was true, she still loved him.

"One night she just disappeared," Larry recalls. "I was dumbfounded and beside myself with concern." But it seemed that no one knew anything. The school informed him that it would be better for him to resign. So he packed his bags and flew to Hong Kong.

Nearly a year later, back in California, Larry received a call from a young Chinese man who had come to study in the United States. He knew Meihong, and he had a message from her for Larry, along with her telephone number.

"I love you!" Larry blurted out when Meihong answered the phone, and she burst into tears.

Larry quickly returned to China, and they were married in Zhenjiang, the city where Pearl Buck had once lived. They were given a wedding gift—a mandarin orange, memorable for its simplicity—by two hotel desk clerks who were caught up in the romance of their story. But the drama wasn't yet finished. Larry had to rush back to the United States in order to meet his visa deadline.

Finally, against the better judgment of his friends but with the assistance of U.S. government officials, the State Department, and local legislators, Larry procured a passport for Meihong. On the first day of the following year, she arrived on American soil. "I just want to live a quiet life now," she said as she fell into the arms of her elated husband.

### ஒ Cupid says:

Sometimes, in order to find love, you have to go against everything you *think*, every bit of rational information. You must follow your heart rather than your head. Every couple has its own set of circumstances to surmount. Though few couples have as dramatic a story as Meihong and Larry's, many have to deal with a difference in culture or country, age or politics. Meihong and Larry believed the best about each other and disregarded the worst that others tried to make them accept. Trust, patience, persistence, and understanding were their guiding angels.

~ 16 ~

# Have I Got the Woman for You!

"Wanted: Healthy married men between the ages of 60 and 80 . . ."
So began the ad in the local newspaper. No, it wasn't signed
"Lonely in L.A." or "Hungry in Hawaii." Rather, it went on to clar-
ify that such men were needed ". . . as volunteers for a study on
healthy aging." It listed the local health center's phone number.
True, Mike and Martha weren't exactly married, but they *had* lived
together for fifteen years. Plus, it was an opportunity for a free
medical exam for Mike. He called the health center.

During his first visit it became clear that the study focused on
male sexual functioning. Mike's dreams and sleep patterns were
monitored; frequency of sexual arousal and intercourse were logged.
He was getting a clean bill of health at no cost, and he found the research interesting.

~ ~ ~

Four months later, Mike was called to the office of a Dr. Smithson, who explained that she was a psychologist connected to the study and would check him for depression and his overall state of emotional health.

"I'm afraid I may be here under false pretenses," Mike confessed to Dr. Smithson. "My long-term relationship ended last month, so now I *really* don't qualify as a married man."

"Since I've scheduled the next three hours for an interview with you, let's just go ahead and use it," she told him.

One thing became immediately clear to Dr. Smithson: this man wasn't wasting any time in figuring out what type of woman he wanted to meet next. As this topic was foremost in his concerns, she decided to question him about it; describing what he wanted in a woman would speak volumes about the man himself, while keeping him free from self-consciousness.

"She has to be warm and affectionate," Mike said as he began his tally of requirements. "I want a woman who had a good relationship with her mother and, therefore, feels a sense of security within herself.

"She should be someone who has a healthy relationship with her children, so she won't be burdened by guilt."

As Mike thoughtfully but unhesitatingly conjured the image of his dream woman that morning, Dr. Smithson kept feeling the presence of her closest friend. *He's describing Jane!* she said to herself.

"Flexibility is very important," he continued, "both emotionally and professionally, because I love to travel and I'd want her to go with me."

*I couldn't possibly tell him about Jane. It would be unethical.*

"She has to be a successful career woman of independent means so she won't be after me for my money. But she can't be too successful, because I would feel uncomfortable with a woman who had more money than me."

*Still, he's only a research volunteer and out of the study now. Anyway, I'll never see him again.*

Dr. Smithson weighed her options:

1. I won't say anything about Jane. (But then two people who may be destined for each other will never meet.)
2. I'll tell him about her, but I won't introduce them. (That would be cruel.)
3. I won't tell Mike, but I'll tell Jane and let her decide. (Jane would never make the first move.)
4. I'll invite them both to a party at my house and subtly introduce them. (That's going too far!)
5. I'll slip Jane's name and number inside his coat pocket. (It might get lost.)
6. I'll give Mike Jane's number and advise her that he might call. (Yes!)

Mike received the information about Jane enthusiastically. Dr. Smithson seemed especially sensitive and kind. He trusted her instincts. And what could he lose?

"You what!?" shrieked Jane on the other end of the line.

"You heard me! He'll be calling you tonight," said Dr. Smith-son. "Just be open. At least meet him for lunch."

"Well," laughed Jane, "if he turns out to be an ax murderer, we'll know your psychological insight sucks!"

As Mike and Jane sat across from each other, a candle flickering between them, Mike began his interviewing process: "How was your relationship with your mother?" he asked between bites of grilled salmon.

"It seems to me the healthiness of my relationship with my fa-ther should be more important to you," chided Jane. "Besides," she continued in her straightforward manner, "you shouldn't tell women what you are looking for, because then they'll just pretend to be what you want."

Candor and pluck were qualities he hadn't mentioned to Dr. Smithson, but they were becoming irresistible in this attractive woman before him. However, he began to let her know in no uncer-tain terms that he was his own man, that he'd had lots of women, that he wasn't capable of deep bonding, and that he had promised himself a year alone, filled with adventures, and wasn't going to let any woman come along and change those plans!

Was he?

Three months later Dr. Smithson received a beautiful silver bracelet from Mike, along with a note that said: "Thank you for giving me the best present I've ever received."

ᨠᩅ Cupid says:

The past doesn't necessarily define the present. Many
women prefer men in their middle years or older. Because
the human sex drive seems to diminish somewhat with age,
an entire world of romance opens up to the middle-aged—
possibly for the first time for those men whose world was
previously occupied solely by lust. Like cognac, men and
women improve with age. You get the best of each other.

# Since We're Neighbors,
# Let's Be Friends

When she was a child, Natalie had written in her diary, "Someday I'm going to marry a boy named Christopher, because I like that name."

One summer evening, after leaving the publishing offices of Holt, where she worked as an editor, Natalie walked home with a bundle of groceries and rode up in the elevator with a man carrying an army reserve uniform. He was friendly, she was open, and they chatted, disembarking on the same floor. When, perhaps an hour later, there was a knock at the door, Natalie wasn't surprised to see her elevator companion. With a broad smile, he asked to borrow an eggbeater. Now, there aren't *that* many uses for an eggbeater, but, curious by nature, Natalie asked, "What for?"

"We need to whip the cream for our strawberry shortcake!" came the reply.

"Sure, you can have it as long as I get some of the finished product," Natalie bargained. He invited her over to his friend's place for dessert and introduced her to the friend . . . Christopher. "She comes with the eggbeater," he explained.

"The moment I walked in and met him, I knew I would marry him," says Natalie today. Adds Christopher, "She just married me for my name. It took five years, but I pursued her until I said yes," he deadpans.

### ॐ Cupid says:

Make friends with your neighbors. You never know when you will need a flashlight, a dog-sitter, a cup of sugar, or a friendly ear. Reinvent the lost concept of community. Whether you live in an apartment building, a condominium, or a house in the suburbs, learn your neighbors' names. Find out where they work and what their hobbies are. Invite them over for dinner. Have an apartment or block party on New Year's Eve, the Fourth of July, Memorial Day. You won't necessarily fall in love with a neighbor, but chances are you will definitely feel more secure in your home and more content in your heart. And you never know to what relative or friend your neighbor might introduce you.

~ 18 ~

# The Emperor's Clothes

The Chilean author of *The House of the Spirits* and *Eva Luna*, Isabel Allende, met her second husband while she was on a book tour in the United States promoting her second novel, *Of Love and Shadows*. Recently divorced after twenty-five years of marriage, Isabel wasn't thinking about remarriage.

Initially, Willie had been intrigued by Isabel's writing, her fiery passion and intelligence shining through on every page—just as they shone in her eyes when he finally met her at a lecture and book signing in northern California. Within a few short weeks Isabel and Willie were living together, and they were married soon thereafter.

About meeting Willie, Isabel says, "If I'd visualized the perfect man for me, I would have visualized a professor of literature in some English university. A man who smokes a pipe, wears camel-hair turtleneck sweaters, and is very refined and cultivated. I never thought I would fall in love with a man like Willie, who looks just like a sailor. I'm madly in love with this man and think he's perfect for me."

ॐ **Cupid says:**

> Better to have an open mind than to have too many idealizations about the perfect mate. Sometimes we are more concerned with a person's packaging than with the content of the soul. Fantasizing your ideal mate is important, but don't let this keep you from responding to the flesh-and-blood people standing before you.

# The Arrangement

"This is what we get for sending our daughter to an American college," Rani's mother lamented. After all, although Rani had been raised in a conservative family in Punjab, India, one that believed in arranged marriages, she had already declined numerous proposals from parentally approved local boys.

Her eldest sister was already married, leaving just Rani and her younger sister eligible for marriage. However, in a traditional Indian family the younger sister cannot marry before her elder sister does, so it was up to Rani to pave the way. Certain traditions had to be followed, and this was one of the most inflexible.

One day Rani's uncle was talking to her mother about possible mates for Rani. "What about Amar?" he asked.

That had been a sad story. One of Rani's cousins had died when her son Amar was only six months old, and the widower had taken his family far from Punjab to the state of Jammu and Kashmir, where he found work as a civil servant. Rani's family hadn't seen Amar since he was an infant, which had been heartbreaking for Rani's mother because she and Amar's mother had been very close friends through school.

"If Rani marries Amar, we will bring him back into our family," Rani's uncle reasoned.

*A splendid idea*, thought Rani's mother. *Ridiculous*, thought Rani's father when he heard the suggestion. Rani's mother finally prevailed over her husband.

What did Rani think? "I just want to marry a man whose children I will be proud to bear. But no matter *who* he is, I want to see him first, even if he is my cousin!" Rani insisted. A melodrama ensued. Finally Rani's mother agreed to send for Amar, who arrived the following week.

Within three months Rani and Amar were married. After more than fifty years of marriage they moved to the United States, where their two beautiful daughters had been educated. "I got what I wanted," says Rani, "children I am proud of."

ॐ Cupid says:

> Listen to your friends when they have someone in mind for you to meet. A matchmaking third party may have an overview of the two personalities, and thus a lucid perspective. Take the hint and check it out.

~ 20 ~

# See You at the Movies

Janie went to see the film *Meetings with Remarkable Men* and met a remarkable man: her future husband, Peter. She was wearing the traditional clothing of a Nepali woman—beads, boots, dress, "the whole nine yards," she says—because it thematically matched the film, which was based on the psychological autobiography of the same name by the mystic philosopher G. I. Gurdjieff. She had purchased her outfit two months earlier on a trip to Nepal. Peter had taken his own journey to Nepal the following month. Now, back in the States, Peter and Janie, with their new ties to Nepal, had gone to the local movie house.

It was impossible not to pick Janie out of a crowded group, but because she had arrived with another man, Peter waited to speak to her until he saw her standing in the ticket line alone. "I was intrigued by this redheaded woman who was dressed in full Nepalese regalia; and, of course, her outfit contributed my opening line: 'Have you been to Nepal?'"

During the moments before her date returned, Peter and Janie established the quick rapport that often comes between people who discover they share a passion for something, be it film or food, politics or photography. They had five short but sweet minutes before filing into the movie house. And that seemed to be that.

Life, however, had other plans for them. Three days later, in a crowd of thirty-five hundred people, fifty miles from where they had originally met, Peter unknowingly sat one seat removed from Janie. In fact, it was a friend of his (who had also been with him at the movie) who noticed Janie first. "Peter, isn't that the woman from *Remarkable Men* sitting on the other side of you?" the friend asked.

That day she was dressed in a sophisticated pantsuit, and all Peter recognized was her red hair and Texan accent. They were attending a meeting in San Francisco, sponsored by the American Association of Humanistic Psychology. They shared concerns for planetary issues. Janie recalls, "He followed me around from that moment on."

From the inception of their romance, Peter and Janie experienced a solidarity between them. Each had been out of significant relationships for two years, and the timing was right. They felt they were coming together as whole people, rather than looking for someone to fill a hole. "There weren't bells ringing," Janie smiles, adding that a "more mature feeling" was undeniable.

After fourteen years, two children, and "a lot of hard work," theirs has become a remarkable marriage.

ॐ **Cupid says:**

It's easy to look back at your experiences and see how everything fell into place effortlessly, although at the time it seemed far from easy. It is important that you prepare yourself for the partner you wish to bring into your life. The best way to do that is to *become* the person you want to meet. Don't wait until you meet someone to start that exercise program, improve your eating habits, or clean up your finances. Do it now, rather than waiting for someone else to do it for you. Prepare yourself for the gifts life has in store for you.

## ~ 21 ~

# The Flirting Game

After living alone for eight years in a small rural town in northeastern California, Charlotte decided that, having met all the "recycled men" there, she needed a bigger pool. Her goal was to meet her mate by June 1990. That gave her less than one year. She had to work quickly and constructively. She tried the personal ads and increased her networking activities.

Charlotte had met a woman who hosted networking breakfasts for women in the San Francisco Bay area. The same woman also taught classes on how to flirt. What could she lose? After two marriages and then eight years as a single woman, she could use some tips.

Charlotte had begun to believe that everyone is born with a basic assumption about life. Hers was: Either this is it or this isn't it. "The moment I'd meet a man," explains Charlotte, "my normal pattern would be to conclude instantaneously, 'He's it!' or 'He's not it.' That's how I'd lived my life up to that point." Although having this realization about herself didn't automatically change her assumption, it did allow her to keep it from influencing her impressions so easily.

The evening of the flirting class arrived. Charlotte had expected only women as participants, but men began streaming in, and one sat down next to her. His name was Bob. She said to herself, *"He's not it."*

When the class divided into groups of three, Charlotte found herself in a triad with Bob and another woman. "For some reason I found myself defending this man I didn't even know," she recounts. "I even put my hand on his knee, in a familiar gesture, while making a point."

When they were given the task of going outside and flirting with someone on the street, Charlotte boasted aloud, "Oh, that's nothing! I've run through the streets naked in Honolulu." At that revelation Bob's ears pricked up. "I thought, *Who is this woman? She defends me. She runs naked through the streets.* I was looking for an unusual woman, a fun woman, and this one caught my interest," he recalls.

When the teacher instructed the class to invite someone within the group out on a date, Bob knew who his first choice was. On the other hand, Charlotte had already joined the line for "the suave, good-looking European guy that all women fall for." Fortunately, he declined, leaving her free for Bob. But she still thought, *This isn't it.*

Their first date consisted of a sunset walk in the scenic Berkeley hills. "I found that Bob was a very interesting man," Charlotte remembers. "He was easy to talk to, and the better I got to know him, the more I realized our worldviews were similar. I *liked* him." But for the next four months, as they dined and danced and discussed, Charlotte continued to remind herself, *"He isn't it."*

In retrospect, she admits that this attitude actually may have helped their relationship develop because she was less self-conscious or concerned about what he thought of her than she otherwise would have been. Thinking *This isn't it* also allowed her to keep sex at bay.

One evening after a date, as they sat in his Honda Prelude and kissed over the emergency brake, Bob said, "I think you're just going out with me until you meet someone better."

"I was so moved that a man could be so vulnerable," says Charlotte. "He hugged me from my neck to my knees, and I thought, *This is it!*" They have been married now for two years.

### ৪৯ Cupid says:

It is a sweet satisfaction to have the other partner step up and make his or her desire known; it is a wonderful feeling to be chosen. During the past twenty-five years, women have become both more skilled in knowing what they want and more assertive in getting it, but it's lovely to be pursued, too. Everyone runs that old tape of *This is it* and *This isn't it*. Accepting that this tendency exists can help you relax into a state where you are actually able to see the other as a human being—in this moment—rather than as a potential marriage partner or someone with whom you will spend the rest of your life. Delight in the uniqueness of the person before you. Appreciate those first, second, and third encounters; they will never come again.

~ 22 ~

# College Sweethearts

When he was thirteen, Alec decided he wanted to be an accountant. Now, at eighteen, he was beginning his education at a community college outside Chicago. Ever since he was a youngster his sense of humor had been appreciated and encouraged; being funny was his way of relating to the world.

That's what Julie first noticed about Alec in her first class of the day, on the first day of the college year: "He made me laugh."

"Boy, this teacher really takes her job seriously," he quipped about the health instructor who seated her class alphabetically. Because both of their last names began with a "B," Alec's assigned seat was right behind Julie's. "This is like grade school! All we need is an inkwell and pigtails," he told the giggling young woman sitting in front of him. Alec was attracted to her personality. "She had more energy and vibrancy than anyone I'd ever known," he recalls, "and she laughed at my jokes!"

His next class was English, and there again was Julie. Within a month they were dating. "That is, *I* was dating Julie, but Julie was dating a swarm of other guys along with me," Alec clarifies. Whether Julie cooled things off with Alec five months later in order to make up her mind about who she wanted to seriously date (as she now remembers), or whether Alec gave her an ultimatum (as he remembers), they didn't see each other for several months.

When she realized how much she missed him, Julie unexpectedly showed up one day at the ice-cream parlor where Alec was working and asked to see him. "That's funny, he was just here a minute ago," said one of the other employees. Poor Alec, who had seen Julie enter the shop and wasn't ready to confront her, was hiding in the walk-in freezer. "It was only twenty below!" he says, laughing at his self-inflicted punishment. He couldn't stay in the freezer forever, though, and Julie was still there when he stiffly walked up to the counter.

"Are you feeling okay?" Julie asked with concern. "You look a little blue."

A year later Alec and Julie were married, and for twenty-two years humor has been the saving grace of their marriage.

### ଛ Cupid says:

Looking at situations—and people—with a sense of humor can get you through anything. Humor also makes life a lot more fun, and makes you more fun to be around. One of the luxuries of high school or college is that the setting provides an interesting assortment of potential friends. The fun is to pick and choose, trying this one on for the prom and that one on for study hall. As grown-ups, we easily lose the sense of spontaneity and carefree dating that we had as adolescents and young adults. Often friendships become *re-lationships* too fast, quickly losing the freshness and appeal they had when the individuals were first drawn together. Relax, lighten up, chill out. Learn to enjoy a new friend without feeling the need to make her or him your soul mate.

23

# Passover Celebration

Esalen Institute sits overlooking the Pacific Ocean above California's Big Sur coast, the rocky waters below filled with marine life. A romantic place. A place to fall in love.

Passover came early that spring. The wildflowers were already in full bloom and the mountains of Big Sur were covered with lupine, wild peas, California poppies, and columbine.

Sunny lived in Los Angeles but had been teaching at Esalen on and off for many years. After suffering a painful, broken relationship and a series of leg injuries, as well as experiencing more than a year of celibacy, she had made up her mind to spend some quiet time healing her shattered heart and broken bones in the remote sanctuary of Big Sur. Her first months of retreat had been trying, what with rainstorms followed by rock and mud slides; and California Highway 1, her only means to civilization, had been closed half the time. But spring was now here and she let herself slip into its pleasures.

For three months Evan had worked as a builder for Esalen on a special project. After his yearlong separation from a twelve-year marriage, he had benefited from and been restored by the serenity of the grounds, the healthy vegetarian food, and the healing effect of nature. In another week he would be heading off to New York—the state of his birth and the locale of his future employment at a private school.

This year Esalen was providing a Passover Seder for all staff, community members, and visiting program participants who wished to attend. There were a rabbi and cantor present; the tables were filled with candles and the symbolic foods of the ritual, such as matzo, bitter herbs, saltwater, hard-boiled eggs, and wine; and the traditional simple stories were retold. Pesach celebrates deliverance and freedom—freedom *from* and freedom *to*—as well as new births and new beginnings, exemplified by the season of spring itself.

Although all the tables in the dining room were set for the occasion, Sunny was drawn to a table where a lively young girl was sitting who looked to be about eight years old. Her name was Rebekah, and she proved charming and entertaining. Sunny missed her own children, who were off at college. After dinner, when people were moving about and chatting, Rebekah took Sunny by the hand and introduced her to an attractive man who had been sitting at their table. "This is my daddy," she announced. Evan had invited his two daughters to celebrate the Jewish holiday with him.

Sunny had seen Evan around the property and at the baths, but until that moment she had never spoken to him. The two began a several-hours-long conversation. "I felt an intense warmth radiate from her," Evan remembers. "She was a good listener, and I felt immediately comfortable in her presence. But I also knew I was leaving soon."

"I went home that night," says Sunny, "and wrote in my journal: 'Met an attractive and interesting man tonight. Seems very self-absorbed, but there is something stirring between us.'" The "stirring" both excited and unsettled her because, although she wanted contact with a man, the last thing she was seeking was a deep involvement.

The "self-absorption," which Evan now admits accurately described his frame of mind that evening, was the result of his plan to move to New York and take a new job. Although the decision had already been made, he was still troubled by second thoughts. "She sat and listened to me go round in circles. I appreciated her generous ear," he says.

Evan postponed his departure. They came into tangential contact over the following weeks, and Sunny kept an eye on Evan. They would meet occasionally and talk. The week before he was scheduled to leave she invited him to her home for dinner. "I thought he was safe," she laughs. "After all, he was leaving for another state."

The dinner evolved into four days during which the pair were inseparable. After that weekend Evan postponed his move for another week, then another, then another. That was three years ago, and Evan and Sunny feel that their relationship has been a rebirth and new beginning for them both.

## ❧ Cupid says:

Religious or national holidays are a great time to meet someone new. Usually a family you know or someone in your community will host a gathering. If no one else does, plan an event yourself; be willing to invite new acquaintances or strangers who would be alone that day, to set an extra place at the table and leave the door open for that last-minute guest. Even if the love of your life doesn't walk through the door, your generosity will bring good cheer to others.

# 24

# One Hundred Love Sonnets

What could be more romantic for a woman than finding a man who writes daily poems of love to her? That's what Riane Eisler found in David. Riane, the author of the seminal work *The Chalice and the Blade*, which attempts to deconstruct the heterosexual relationship, had been divorced for several years after a fifteen-year marriage. She had nearly given up on the possibility of meeting a man with whom she could create a full partnership—someone who would be a real friend. Friendship, after all, is the avenue to equality.

~ ~ ~

David had been at a loss, knocking around like a pinball, in the lonely wasteland of Los Angeles. His secretary grew increasingly concerned when she saw him shuffle into the office one afternoon after another unsuccessful affair. "I'm typing a manuscript for a *wonderful* woman who I think you should meet," she told him.

"She's quite attractive, very, very bright, and interested in the future." It all sounded good to David, a systems scientist, psychologist, and futurist.

"And she's interested in art and music," the secretary continued.

"My God, this sounds too good to be true," he laughed.

When she said, "She's a lawyer," his image of the woman began to deflate slightly. "And she's writing a book on divorce," she added. He noticeably tensed up. But when the secretary said, "Her name is Riane Eisler," he was "instantly put on guard and for some crazy reason thought of Adolf Eichmann, the killer of Jews." He said to himself, *I'll never go near that one*, though he told his secretary, "Yes, she sounds like a possibility."

A year passed. Every so often he'd come dragging into the office from yet another romantic disappointment and the secretary would prod him, saying, "You really ought to call Riane Eisler."

"Oh, yeah, yeah, that one, sure." Naturally he'd never quite get around to making that call.

≈ ≈ ≈

"Hello. Is Elizabeth there?" a fetching voice asked David, who, one day, in the absence of his secretary, answered the phone.

"No, she isn't. Who may I say called," he asked curiously.

"Riane Eisler."

*This can't be the same Riane Eisler I know so well in my stereotype*, he thought. But he kept her on the line chatting. One thing led to another, and before he knew it they'd made a date to meet for lunch in three days.

"Both of us were absolutely fascinated with each other," remembers Riane. "We walked all over Westwood Village, excitedly sharing thoughts and experiences." To his great relief, David discovered that Riane was definitely *not* related to Eichmann. In fact, she and her family had been forced to flee from Germany because they were Jews.

Riane had an appointment with her accountant late that afternoon, but she met David again for dinner that evening. "I went home after dinner and wrote my first love poem," says David, sparkling from the memory. He was so eager to give the poem to her that, at four o'clock in the morning, he taxied over to her apartment and dropped the envelope through the mail slot in her front door.

Riane never suspected that the poem awaiting her the next morning would be the first of one hundred. She read:

*To Riane*

Who are you? This girl
I dallied a day with
and held a portion
of the night?
Something in you seems
to speak to me out
of a past beyond
remembering, or
from a future

too far ahead
to yet behold.
Who are you with
the elfin smile
and soft hands?
Why do I love you
so intensely
so quickly?

## ঌ Cupid says:

Stereotyping is dangerous, and history is filled with examples of how it can be lethal. At best, categorizing people causes you to miss out on many enriching experiences; at worst, it ignites genocide.

Just as men have been known to stereotype women, women are sometimes guilty of stereotyping men. How many times have you heard the dictum "All men are the same" or "Men only want one thing"? The next time you have that thought, remember this: on the whole, men want what women want—to be loved and appreciated, to be safe and nurtured, to live a stimulating, fruitful life, to find true partnership. Men are not the enemy.

# 25

# When Dreams Come True

The recurring dream seemed real and mystical at once, something out of a gothic novel. There were no words, only the image of a woman's face—an attractive woman with long dark hair. It haunted his nights and pursued him in mirror and glass reflections throughout the day. It wasn't frightening, just persistent. Gary, the keeper of the dream, thought the image resembled country-and-western singer Loretta Lynn and wondered if the message meant that he would meet her or work with her in some capacity. He was certain that the beckoning woman was an announcement from his subconscious that he would soon meet his life partner.

Three months into the dreams, he was asked to teach at an institute in Arizona for the summer. In June, convinced that he would meet *her* there, Gary made a grand public declaration at his first seminar: "This is where I will find the person with whom I am to be in relationship." Every single woman in attendance thought *she* must be this person.

Kathleen had been invited by a friend on the board of directors of the same institute to attend the special summer session. Because Kathleen was to be away in India for three months, she wasn't going to be able to take part in the institute's program, but she promised to attend the closing-day ceremony in September. She and her friend had also begun making early plans for Thanksgiving. "You have to set a place for my boyfriend," Kathleen had insisted—even though she didn't currently *have* a boyfriend.

The decisive hour of the closing day of that summer's program arrived. As Gary was privately realizing that he might yet have to eat his words about meeting his dream woman, unbeknownst to him a willowy woman in her forties with long dark hair and bangs entered the lecture hall where he was presenting his last talk.

*How interesting the man seems, how full of heart*, Kathleen thought as she observed him and listened to his words. *Yes, I'd like to meet him.*

There are an abundance of dark-haired women in the world, so when one more approached Gary, introducing herself and asking for a hug, he didn't stop to think, *This could be the one!* It was the embrace that shook him into recognition. There was a rush of energy from the base of his spine to the top of his head.

The experience wasn't associated with lust. Kathleen now describes it as "a bursting from the heart." Gary stepped back from her, put his hand to his chest, and repeated, "My heart, my heart!" Fortunately for them both, it wasn't a coronary; it was love.

He walked over to a waiting car, and she swooned her way over to a grassy area to catch her breath. Oops! He didn't know the name of this dark-haired mystery woman or how to contact her or anything about her, but he knew he recognized her from his dreams.

"Can you wait five minutes?" he implored his companions. Running back toward the spot where their hearts had met, he told her, "I have no idea who you are or what you do. I live in Denver, but I don't have to. When can I come and see you?" They set a date for three weeks later in Los Angeles, where Kathleen lived. Once home, they talked on the phone two or three times a day, gathering important data, practical and personal, in order to learn as much as they could about each other.

Kathleen knew she was totally in love with him. When she went to pick him up at the airport, she was embarrassed not to recognize him. She remembers thinking, *So that's what you look like, this time*— as if they had known each other before.

Three weeks later she visited Gary in Denver, where they set a wedding date for September of the following year. Their third "date" was at Kathleen's friend's house that Thanksgiving. A place setting for Gary had, of course, already been set aside.

## ᐧᐧ Cupid says:

> Dreams—both day and night—are messages from the soul, maps of the human heart. Listen to them and you will learn

a lot about yourself and what you are looking for in a mate. Life is full of surprises, and will unfold naturally and gracefully if you allow it. As long as you struggle to control your life, focusing on certain outcomes, you will be disappointed. Let your motto be: Let Go and Let Love.

# 26

# A Woman of Independence

Ellen had finally reached a point in her life where she felt a deep satisfaction with who she was and with her stimulating job as a publishing executive. And she felt a peaceful acceptance of her life as a single woman. Even though she was in her mid-thirties and had never been married, her sense of identity didn't revolve around an association with a man, as it did for so many of her women friends. In fact, she relished her independence: there was no one she had to take care of, no one to be concerned about when she worked late at the office. Yes, autonomy suited her just fine. She could pick up at any moment and do whatever she wanted.

After his separation, Ivan waited about fifteen seconds to start dating again. He felt an exciting new sense of freedom in his life, the liberty to be with someone else or to be alone—as he was that balmy summer night at the Lincoln Center Mostly Mozart concert. Although Ivan was a medical doctor and a professor, his interests were well-rounded, his two great passions being music and literature.

During intermission he noticed the attractive woman in the red dress and kept a steady but discreet eye on her to make sure she was alone before he approached her. They chatted briefly before the intermission bell sounded, and he impulsively asked her if she would like to meet for coffee after the concert.

Ivan exuded a kind of European charm, stylish and urbane. Ellen had a quick wit and an exceptional ability to articulate her rare intelligence. Her conversation conveyed a semi-ingenuelike quality, a willingness to see the best in people, which formed an interesting counterpoint to her broad sophistication. Neither of them had patience with idle talk, and at the nearby deli they easily took their conversation to points of personal history and philosophical quandaries. They would definitely see one another again. How about next week's concert in Central Park? It's a deal!

*Who* is *this man?* Ellen asked herself the following week in the park as Ivan began unloading onto his favorite table linens the feast that Zabar's had assembled. But it was the flash of the fireflies glimmering against the antique sterling silver that took her breath away. He'd brought his family heirlooms!

"If you take such exquisite care with a *picnic*, I envy your patients!" she laughed. And, indeed, that night she became his patient herself, in a way. A recently acquired case of poison ivy was driving her mad. Was there any relief to be had? After the concert they drove to a pharmacy, where Ivan solicitously scouted out the best cortisone cream for her skin and whipped out his prescription pad to procure an oral antidote.

After he dropped Ellen off at her apartment—naturally, walking her to the door and waiting until she was safely inside—she luxuriated in the feeling that she had been courted that night. His genuine concern for her comfort, his attentiveness toward her, his confidently assured yet nurturing temperament seemed almost anachronistic. Rather than living in Manhattan in 1974, they could have been in Vienna in 1874 or Paris in 1912. He was a romantic. A true gentleman.

There might be room for a man in her life after all.

### ℰ Cupid says:

Often, when you least expect it, Mr. or Ms. Wonderful comes waltzing into your life. What probably made you most appealing was an ability to independently enjoy your life, with or without a partner. Western society is oriented toward couples, and it takes a concerted effort to become contented as a single person, especially if you're a woman. And you can't fake it. Having the willingness to venture out on your own—be it to dinner, a concert, or a foreign country—takes conviction and practice. But once you have acquired this skill, your life is truly your own.

## ～ 27 ～

# Written in the Stars

They were both Virgos and met shortly after their birthdays one September. A long-term mutual friend who was a psychologist and astrologer had watched each of them rise and fall with the current of stormy relationships and, for years, had thought Coeleen and Ed, both in their fifties, should meet.

"I was impressed because this friend is very critical of men. So when she held Ed in such high regard, I knew he must be a pretty exceptional male," Coeleen says. During that same time, Coeleen had two housemates who were in a Ph.D. program, and she would often hear them speaking favorably about one of their psychology instructors—a man named Ed. *It couldn't possibly be the same one*, Coeleen thought to herself. "It couldn't possibly be the same one," her housemates assured her.

Of course, it *was* the same Ed. He took the initiative and called Coeleen, who, aware of the three "references" and many synchronicities, then wrote him a letter, prompting a response. When it arrived, she remembers thinking, *All right, this looks like a generous man who accepts responsibility and pays attention to detail. I'll meet him.*

In past relationships, Coeleen felt, she had not chosen particularly well for herself. Now she asked for guidance to help her know what she *needed* rather than be seduced by what she thought she wanted. Still, she warned herself not to set up too many expectations.

Since they lived in cities eighty miles apart, Coeleen suggested she meet Ed in front of the old, elegant movie house—the only movie house—on Main Street in a charming town midway between them. "You can't miss it!" she assured him.

"I cruised into Saratoga feeling reasonably confident that I knew what a movie theater and a box office and a marquee would look like," Ed jokes, "secure that I could find the one movie theater on Main Street!

"So I drove up and down Main Street two or three times," he continues. "But I could not find anything that resembled a movie house." Wondering if it might be somehow obscured, he parked and began walking up and down the street. Though he could find no theater, he did spot a vacant lot with just the beginning of construction on it.

Meanwhile, dressed in her flashy fuchsia linen suit ("I'd thought, *If the guy can handle my fuchsia linen suit, he's okay*"), Coeleen had parked her car and gone looking for the town's famous landmark. "It wasn't there!" she laughs. "It had been torn down. All I saw was a big empty lot with the beginning of a foundation on it. The first thing that hit me was that this relationship was *not* going to be movie material. I told myself to let go of the idea of a Hollywood romance." Her second thought was about the foundation, which symbolized to her a new beginning—"starting from scratch," as she puts it.

Thinking that perhaps the theater was hidden behind the construction, Ed started walking toward it. "And then I saw a lady in a bright pink dress sitting on the wall of the construction and thought, *Could this be her?* It was a Saturday night, and you don't see many single people on the street, especially in our age range," he says. Ed was favorably impressed with the fuchsia suit.

They went to a local restaurant for dinner, and as they were gathering information about each other, Coeleen felt guarded and concluded that they were more likely to become friends than lovers. She was impressed, though, by the fact that Ed was maintaining a household for his aging father, an adult daughter, and his grandson, as well as a full-time practice in psychiatry. Later in the evening they went to hear some jazz, and once or twice she caught him looking at her out of the corner of his eye.

When they said good-bye, Coeleen thought, *This is a man who could be a good friend.* But she says now that as she drove the thirty miles home, "it began to dawn on me that this was the person I was supposed to be open to. I felt that a soul mate had entered my life."

A week later, Coeleen made it very clear to Ed that she wanted to be in a relationship with him. His response? "He sounded like he'd said yes about ten years before," Coeleen smiles.

They worked out, in his words, "a wonderful system of migra-tion": during the next three and a half years they alternated weekends

at each other's homes. Ed's natural ability to nurture and be supportive was what ultimately won Coeleen's heart. He cleaned out a spare
room in his house for Coeleen to use as an art studio. It was important for her to do her own work even when they were together. She
says, "I'd always done my art *in spite of* my relationships, but when
someone came along and said, 'I want to make a place for you to do
your work,' it was the answer to my dreams."

> ### ಶ Cupid says:
>
> Pray or meditate for guidance in choosing a partner best
> suited to be your friend and lover. "[Prayer] doesn't help
> God, it helps me," says the C. S. Lewis character in *Shad-
> owlands.* You pray and meditate as a means of contacting
> what is truest and deepest within yourself, what is *really*
> best for you, rather than what your senses tell you you
> want.

## ~ 28 ~

# The Cook, the Restaurant, the Waitress, and Her Boyfriend

This was no *Frankie and Johnny* diner dive; it was class. It was Chez Panisse. Mima had been waitressing her way through the University of California at Berkeley in comparative literature and her second language, French. Although she was living with her boyfriend, that Monday morning when Tom, the new cook, walked in she began "lusting after him."

They worked together during the day, with him filling her orders, and they catered together at night. It was inevitable that they would take that one drink too many one night after work. Sitting at a table, Mima ("I was very forward") looked Tom in the eye and murmured, "You know, I've been wanting to kiss you for a long time." If the answer is in a kiss, she found it. And it was positive.

After that, it was sneaking kisses out on the back porch and exchanging notes behind the counter, although Tom remembers, "I was cautious, still thinking about a disappointing earlier relationship. I was serious about my work and kept to myself."

Six months later, Tom moved on to a new restaurant, and Mima, after graduating, moved to the other side of the counter, as a cook. A year later, Tom moved in with Mima. A year after that, they decided to try their skill at their own food business near Santa Cruz, California. They opened a charming American charcuterie called Carried Away, specializing in take-out.

Seven years after they'd met at Chez Panisse, they were married. Mima jokes, "People ask, 'What could be so romantic about being in business together that would make you want to get married?' That's not the idea. It's not that it's so romantic; it's that we finally got around to it. We finally had a little time and a little money and the energy to do it."

## ࡪ Cupid says:

Food and sex are two of the most consistently consuming passions of humankind. Knowing this makes it easy to understand why so many couples meet either working in or dining at restaurants. My great-aunt Cupid used to say: "The way to a woman's heart is through her heart. The way to a man's heart is still through his stomach." Ethnic and regional cooking classes have become very popular ways to spend an evening socially. You can learn to make Japanese sushi, Thai coconut and chicken soup, Moroccan couscous, Indian curries, French bouillabaisse, Spanish paella, or vegetarian feasts. Read *The Art of Eating* by M. F. K. Fisher and see the movie *Like Water for Chocolate*. Then you'll know why food is sexy and sex is edible.

# Love of a Salesman

When the six-foot-two salesman approached Christina she noticed a swagger to his walk. "I tried to avoid him because he seemed so overconfident," she remembers. But John had noticed her the moment she stepped through the front door of the shop, and he made a beeline for this "fresh, innocent-looking" college student.

"I was there to buy a bike, not to find a boyfriend. I already had a boyfriend," laughs Christina. The salesman turned out to be the owner of the shop, "but he didn't even understand the principles of how to operate a bike pump!" she jokes with feigned exasperation. However, John's skills at salesmanship won the day, and Christina left the shop as the proud owner of a new bicycle.

"Fortunately, adjustments to the bike had to be made," says John. "I knew she'd be back to pick it up." The following week Christina came to claim her purchase. Of course the adjustments hadn't been made yet, and John invited her into his office for the two-hour wait.

"She had such a sunny disposition; she was so bright and funny. It felt good just to be in her presence," he recalls. John needed a bit of sunshine in his life. Compared with most of the people he had met in Minneapolis, he felt more independent, experienced, sophisticated—"pretentious," he now calls it. True, he had traveled the globe during the summers when he was free from boarding school, and he had left home in England when he was a tender fifteen and been making his own way ever since. But something had happened to him in this midwestern landscape out of Norman Rockwell: he felt jaded. When a breath of fresh air in the form of Christina burst forth into his life, he wasn't going to let it breeze on by so easily.

"I had my schoolbooks with me, but I ended up listening to John's adventure stories of time spent living in Africa with his father, who was a civil engineer, and other worldly travels. I found him fascinating and eloquent," says Christina. Two hours later her bike was ready, but before John could ask for her telephone number she was out the door—possibly never to be seen by him again.

John waited several months, but the sparkling nineteen-year-old never reappeared. Entrepreneurial by nature, John devised a scheme that he hoped would bring Christina back into his shop: at Christmastime he would send out coupons good for 25 percent off to all his customers. John gave the store manager a description of Christina, along with strict instructions to call him if she was spotted.

The ploy worked: in walked Christina with a pair of ice skates nonchalantly thrown over her shoulder; she had just skated across the frozen lake to the sale. She was glad to have an excuse to visit the bike shop again, for during the several months that had passed since she met John she had thought of him daily. "When he never called I figured he wasn't as interested as he had seemed initially," she says. The manager called John, who with great relief invited Christina out for lunch, vowing to himself never to lose her again.

Their friendship developed over time and Christina completed her university schooling. They have been married for thirteen years now and still find each other fresh and fascinating.

### ❧ Cupid says:

In many first meetings there is an element of instant empathy—a palpable chemical or gut reaction between the two people. Love seems a random, chance occurrence. To mentally construct the personality and physical qualities of a fantasy lover may be an enjoyable pastime, but when you are hit by Cupid's arrow, your heart is no longer your own.

~ 30 ~

# The Auteur and His Muse

It was a Saturday afternoon. On Saturdays Henry's secretary had the day off, so he opened his own mail and answered his own telephone. He'd been working tirelessly on editing his newest film, about a group of Los Angeles women who, in spite of their professional successes, all had eating disorders.

After opening the mail—most of which went into the garbage— Henry went back to the editing room. Many exhausting hours later, Henry suddenly thought, *What was that? What* was *that!* Racing down to his office, he began going through the wastebasket, which held that afternoon's discarded pieces of mail, "like a crazy man."

"What was that?" he repeated over and over to himself. He realized he didn't even know what he was looking for. Opening crumpled, rejected pieces of paper, he came across one that had an inexplicable urgency about it, although he had no idea why. It was an invitation to the opening of a Clifford Odets play starring a woman he didn't know named Victoria. He received dozens of invitations a week for film, theater, and art openings. What *was* it about this card?

He called the number listed, and an intriguing female voice answered. Announcing who he was, he admitted he didn't know why he'd felt compelled to call. It turned out that Henry's name and identity were known to Victoria but she had never seen any of his films. She had routinely sent out invitations for the opening of the play to hundreds of casting agents, producers, and, yes, directors.

Henry and Victoria began asking each other questions and laughing at one another's answers. "You, too?" they responded as they marveled at their similarities. They had a five-hour conversation that night . . . four hours the next night . . . and six the next.

After fifteen hours of telephone conversation, he knew he was in love and so did Victoria, who says, "I had been looking for my twin, and with Henry I felt totally known."

Later that week, they met in person, at the rough-cut screening of his film. By the end of the screening she realized Henry was just what she was looking for: "Someone with whom I could share all of myself—like a best girlfriend I could have sex with."

On their first dinner date they felt that they already knew well the particulars about each other's lives; he'd been wanting children, she'd been wanting children. When Victoria said, "I just want you to be happy," Henry blurted out, "Then have my baby!"

"After years of waiting for each other, we didn't believe in wasting time," laughs Victoria.

Two years later, Papa Henry, Mama Victoria, and Baby Sabrina are all doing well. And expecting a baby boy to join the family soon!

### 🦆 Cupid says:

Sometimes you have to go through the garbage in life in order to find what's really important to you. We live in a society addicted to instant gratification. It takes time, patience, and willingness to get to know someone you've invited into your life. Take the time in the early moments and days of a new relationship to savor this unique person. Find out all you can about the person's likes and dislikes, childhood and dreams. What makes him laugh? What does her voice remind you of? Is it a turn-on?

Remember when you were in high school and spent hours on the phone with your boyfriend or girlfriend, and your mother kept telling you to start your homework? Now you can talk as long as you want, there's no homework waiting, and love is still just as sexy on the phone as it used to be—the original safe sex. It's a wonderful way to get to know someone: you cross a lot of boundaries and have a direct pipeline to the pure essence, the most relaxed version of the other person.

# The Gospel of Love

Large cities can be isolating and alienating. Isn't it ironic that the most populated areas may also be the most lonely? One's solitude becomes crowded with loneliness. People are fearful of verbal or physical assault and therefore lose a natural openness to and curiosity about strangers.

Jean was living in Manhattan with a roommate. A woman in her thirties, Jean had withdrawn from the world because of something deeper, more serious: a feeling of existential angst that ate away at her like saltwater on an anchor.

One Sunday morning, Jean's roommate invited her to attend service at Saint Ignatius's Episcopal Church. The church was within walking distance of their Upper West Side apartment, and it was a lovely early summer day. Jean loved a variety of music, and she found herself looking forward to listening to the choir and, as a lapsed Catholic, to experiencing once again the sounds of Gregorian chant and the Mass recited in Latin.

~ ~ ~

The choir loft is an especially convenient place from which to spot an attractive newly enlisted parishioner. Rick noticed Jean from above before the religious observance began and managed to catch her eye several times during the service. "He looks like a cute boy," Jean whispered to her roommate. *But he's too young for me*, she thought resignedly.

Afterward, both Rick and Jean went to the coffee hour in hopes of meeting each other. Their brief interchange made a deep impression, but any further contact would have to wait until Rick returned from a summer abroad in Europe.

Jean liked the feeling of community generated at St. Ignatius's. It offered the best of what she remembered from her childhood church experiences and a satisfying social outlet with like-minded people. She looked forward to autumn.

There is some confusion about who asked whom out to a movie that Sunday in September. In any case, rather than spend a blazing Indian-summer afternoon inside a dark theater, they walked for hours in Central Park amid trees covered with leaves that shone like garnets and rubies and amber when the sun caught them. Jean found Rick's playfulness and whimsical take on life very attractive. But he was also a serious—and in fact quite brilliant—composer and musician.

And what a voice! Rick was full of surprises that afternoon, not the least of which was his invitation to Jean to attend his satirical musical, *Le Cri de l'Aubergine* ("The Cry of the Eggplant"), opening the following week. Jean found the metaphor of this "vegetable tragedy" hilarious. And when Rick began speaking French onstage, Jean's defenses toppled. She gladly fell in love.

### 🐦 Cupid says:

Refuge from a hostile world comes in many forms. So do religious sanctuaries. A temple of worship is a natural place to connect with those who have similar religious and/or spiritual values. You may prefer a shrine or a stupa, a pagoda or a tabernacle, to a synagogue, cathedral, or mosque. On college campuses you can find religious centers for many denominations. The particular affiliation is less important than the desire for a spiritual and human connection. As Victor Hugo said, "A church is God between four walls." The ability to believe in love once again, to believe in goodness, is a gift that cannot be measured.

## ~ 32 ~

# Runners' Match

John had been a member of the Turtle Island Singles, a group of long-distance runners, for two months before Ted ran that day's annual six-kilometer Labor Day race. He didn't notice Ted until the halfway mark, when he was suddenly striding next to "the most shapely legs I'd ever seen on a man."

Slowing down to a jog, John asked how he was enjoying the race and introduced himself. He'd recently stopped smoking, Ted said, and hoped to discipline his body back into shape by running. They agreed to meet at the champagne brunch that was to follow the race.

Although John hadn't joined the group solely because it could provide him with an opportunity to meet available men, this consideration had colored his decision. Now he was glad he had joined. On the other hand, Ted *had* joined the club with the intention of meeting a mate.

During the brunch they discovered that music was a shared passion: John had a baby grand in his living room, and Ted was an amateur opera singer. They also discovered they both had grown children and loved to travel. Soon thereafter they quit the Turtle Island Singles and joined the Rocky Mountain Runners—an organization for couples.

### ❧ Cupid says:

Joining singles clubs is a sure way to meet new people. There are singles groups for lovers of sports, foreign languages, dance, animals, literature, computers, cooking, travel, nature, and music. If an organization you belong to doesn't have a singles branch, take the initiative and start one. You will be providing a service not only for yourself but for many others as well.

~ 33 ~

# Great Expectations

In Japan, women are traditionally married by their mid-twenties. Yoko, a modern, independent woman who was past thirty, grew more concerned about her single status as time passed. "Friends had suggested the dating service before to me, but I never trusted it," she remembers.

One morning Yoko awakened and decided to take a chance on the contemporary version of a matchmaker. *I have nothing to lose, and, maybe, a husband to gain*, the gambler in her thought. The next day the computer spewed out a list of four possible matches who had already shown interest in Yoko's video introduction.

Somewhat arbitrarily she chose one ("I liked his eyes"), and they met for dinner the next week. "I couldn't stand him that night. He didn't seem like the kind of assertive man I thought I was looking for," recalls Yoko.

Hiroshi had a very different response: "I knew immediately that I wanted to marry her."

He pursued and she rebuffed. Eventually, her heart softened to his overtures, and they were married six months later.

🐦 Cupid says:

Be willing to give someone you've met a second chance. Sometimes the sleepers are the real winners. Look closely at what it is that bothers you about the person. Is it something within you that you are projecting onto her or him? Are your expectations unfair and unrealistic? Are you seeing the person for who he or she really is?

## ~ 34 ~

# The Catholic Worker

Father Larry had been raised in a large Irish Catholic family in San Francisco. He'd come from privilege and he knew it. Before religion became big business, one of its core precepts was to feed, clothe, and shelter the poor, to care for the less fortunate. As a child Larry had been inculcated with this philosophy, so it seemed natural to his family when he announced his intention of entering the priesthood. He was duly ordained but soon wearied of the standard life of a parish priest. He longed to be working with people, directly supporting their lives in the tradition of Saint Francis and of Dorothy Day and Peter Maurin, the cofounders of the original Catholic Worker House.

Operating a Catholic Worker House seemed to Father Larry the best way to exemplify Peter Maurin's challenge to become "a go-giver rather than a go-getter." He decided he would provide a home for wayward and unwanted teenagers, those whose family lives had been difficult at best, destructively abusive at worst.

The House, as it came to be known by the locals, was a haven for the have-nots—the destitute, the homeless, the sick, the drug-addicted and alcoholic, the unwed mothers—as well as for those whose only affliction was that they were unwanted. Father Larry welcomed them all.

Less than a year after the doors opened, Ronnie came by one day with her sister Anna (who volunteered at the house) to pick up a young girl and take her out shopping. The meeting between Ronnie and Father Larry seemed inconsequential at the time. He *was*, after all, a Catholic priest; and she, having recently been through the annulment of her first marriage, was working hard at stabilizing her life.

"Hi," Ronnie said, in her friendly but quiet way. *He's a priest!* she inwardly thought. *And he's running a house for teenagers. That makes sense*, she noted facetiously. "He looked different from any priest I'd ever seen before," she recalls.

A few weeks later, at Thanksgiving, Ronnie and Anna were preparing a stuffing and getting ready to dress their turkey when the phone rang. It was Father Larry calling for advice on *his* stuffing for the bird he was preparing for the house members. "Come on over," Anna said. When Father Larry arrived, it was mostly he and Anna who interacted; Ronnie was in her usual mode of staying busy, observing, and listening.

Things evolved rather quickly after that. Ronnie volunteered at the house on a regular basis: she'd bring food or take the teenagers out or help with coverage, which meant she spent long winter evenings in the company of Father Larry. By Christmas he realized he was preoccupied with the dark-haired, soft-spoken woman who gave so generously of her time. When he told her of his concern she said, "I don't know what that means . . . 'preoccupied.'"

"I think I've fallen in love with you," he replied.

"We had a long way to go after that," recalls Ronnie now. Out of necessity, their relationship took on a discreet quality. Neither knew how long they would stay involved or where their involvement would lead. Father Larry continued his active opposition to nuclear weapons, and a year into their liaison he was arrested for protesting at a military site. It was while he was in prison that he realized just how much he loved Ronnie and that "if that meant opening myself up to marrying her, then that was the way it was going to be."

Soon after, Larry resigned from the priesthood. He and Ronnie have been married for over ten years now, and together they still operate the Catholic Worker House.

## ཞ Cupid says:

> The notion of *right livelihood* is important. How you live your life, spend your time, and earn a living may (without your even knowing it) affect a large circle of friends and associates. You may want to meet someone who is living a meaningful life, who makes a contribution to society. But in order to meet such a person you too must be contributing something useful to your community.

# 35

# It Takes Two to Samba

She was tired from a full day at the publishing house. But after dinner, her friend Leslie, whose birthday they were celebrating, insisted they stop at a club on Market Street in San Francisco before ending the night. Amy was confused and a little dazed by a series of disappointing noncommittal relationships, so the last thing on her mind was meeting her mate at the Latin dance club she soon found herself in.

Steve says he noticed her the moment she entered the room. Reeling from having terminated a dead-end relationship himself, Steve was the opposite of gun-shy: he was *ready* to meet the woman of his dreams. And somehow he knew that she was standing there. Before she had a chance to sit down he charmed her to the dance floor, where they sambaed till the final beat of the conga drums faded.

The next morning when Amy arrived at her office an enormous bouquet of white tulips awaited her. The day after that it was red roses. Then it was daffodils.

Seven months later Amy and Steve moved into the upstairs Victorian flat they now share. He still sends her flowers.

ॐ Cupid says:

> Dancing is good for what ails the lonely or brokenhearted. It's hard to be unhappy when you're having fun! Go to a dance club with a friend or group of friends and take dance lessons. Learn folk, tango, ballroom, Cajun, tap, square, swing, or African steps, and dance the blues away.

# 36

# Machismo at Its Best

When they eloped fifty-four years ago, Sam was twenty-three and Bea seventeen. They met in 1939 in Queens, New York, where they both lived in Middle Village. Although their parents knew each other, Sam and Bea had never been formally introduced. Like many young people, they knew each other only by sight. In those days, neighborhoods were still neighborhoods: the houses were modest single-family residences; the streets were safe; robbery in homes was rare; and girls sat gossiping on their porches, which provided a great vantage point from which to flirt with handsome boys as they strolled by in pairs or trios.

"I'd been keeping an eye on Bea for some months," recalls Sam. "All the boys had a go for her, but I challenged anyone to make a pass at her—although it was a little embarrassing because I was several years older than her." With a reputation as a worthy street fighter, Sam found few rivals.

From her perspective Bea considered Sam a "handsomely macho older man. Macho was a *good* thing to be in those days," laughs Bea. "Now it's awful."

As the summer vacation came to an end and Bea returned to school, Sam would meet her bus every afternoon, carry her books, and walk her home. "You're dating a *child*. What's wrong with you?" accused Sam's parents. Bea's weren't much more supportive. Sam and Bea had spoken about marriage, but marriage was not her parents' idea of what she should do with the rest of her life. And living together without being married was simply out of the question for them. Sam says she was such a beauty that he was afraid he might lose her. So . . .

It was Sam's idea, and Bea loved it: they would elope.

A few of his trusted friends helped with the arrangements. One drove them, through a blizzard, to Alexandria, Virginia, where a marriage ceremony could be performed without a waiting period. There was some urgency because the next day was Sam's birthday and he wished to romantically link his future birthday celebrations to his anniversaries. "I'm the best birthday present you'll ever receive," Bea boasted.

The next morning they were married by a justice of the peace and sent a telegram to both their parents: "Got married STOP Be back in a while STOP Letter follows STOP Sam and Beatty."

≈ ≈ ≈

"Are you pregnant?" was the first question that popped out of Bea's mother's mouth.

"No!" came Bea's puzzled and somewhat indignant answer.

"Then why did you get married if you didn't have to?"

Sam stepped up with all the chivalry he could muster and said, "I didn't want to lose her."

Shocked but in the end accepting, both sets of parents "made us a wedding party," laughs Bea. "What could they do?" she shrugs.

All the doubters had to eat their own gossip when Bea "finally" gave birth to her firstborn, Ellen, *eighteen* months later. "My mother is now ninety years old," says Bea, "and she recently gave me that very telegram we sent to her fifty-four years ago."

### ᘓ Cupid says:

A difference in age can bring novelty and a fresh perspective to a relationship. Although Sam was only six years older than Bea, he seemed like an older man to her. The older-man/younger-woman syndrome is thought to be perfectly natural and is taken for granted; yet an older woman attracted to a younger man can arouse considerable comment. Why? Do we carry deep fears of Oedipal consequences? Do we make our own Freudian interpretations? Be less concerned about a person's age than with how you feel in that person's presence and what you can learn from him or her.

## ~ 37 ~

# Book Lovers

Susan was in acupuncture school and needed part-time employment. She loved books and had always wanted to work in a bookstore. Bookshop Santa Cruz seemed like a great place to hang out, and there were always interesting people frequenting the shop. So she put her resume together and set out to visit the lively bookstore.

Kelsey was the first person she met, and she handed over her resume to the responsive woman with the tender blue-gray eyes. Although Kelsey didn't do the hiring herself, she found Susan to be "quite substantial" in both character and experience, and urged the manager to hire her.

The two women found that each day they would eagerly check to see if the other was working; Susan now laughs when she remembers inspecting the employees' new schedule each Friday for an advance notice of Kelsey's shifts. They each felt a nervous attraction toward the other, but hadn't yet placed it in the arena of romance.

After two weeks at the bookstore, Susan knew she had a serious crush on Kelsey and garnered up enough nerve to ask her out to lunch.

"I'll bring burritos," Kelsey offered without hesitation.

"Great. We'll go down to the beach," Susan proposed.

Susan knew she was drawn to what she'd already seen of Kelsey, but she wanted the full scoop on who she was and what she wanted. *And* Susan didn't want to waste any time finding out.

"So," she began the conversation, "are you a lesbian?"

Trying not to choke on her burrito, Kelsey said, "Eyyyess . . ." and wondered what was coming next.

"Are you attracted to me?"

"Uh-huh . . ." Kelsey replied cautiously.

"Why?"

Aware that she was being interviewed for the position of Susan's new lover, Kelsey felt a mixture of intimidation (by Susan's bold approach) and admiration (for her candor and sincerity). Susan's third degree continued until she seemed certain that Kelsey was the woman for her.

"Oh, one last thing," said Susan, her eyes lighting up like a spark plug. "What do you want in a relationship?"

"Friendship, romance, and passion," said Kelsey with calm assurance.

Today, one of Kelsey's favorite images is of Susan—a month after their first lunch date, and after Susan had broken her foot—clumping toward her on crutches across the cobblestoned courtyard of the bookstore, with a luscious lavender rose set securely between her smiling lips.

Kelsey and Susan recently celebrated five years together.

ॐ Cupid says:

> If you are a book lover wanting to meet another book lover, spend time perusing titles in your favorite neighborhood bookstore. Many of the independently owned operations offer nightly guest lectures and readings by locally, nationally, and even internationally known thinkers and writers. You can often find comfortable chairs; some bookshops even have cafés that allow customers to enjoy tea or cappuccino. You might make a new friend, and you can pick up some interesting reading material and support your local bookstore at the same time.

~ 38 ~

# The French Fisherman's Catch

Sarah bicycled the eighty miles from Rennes to Port-Louis on a rainy day in May. She was on a four-month photography and bike-riding tour along the west coast of Brittany.

Halfway to Port-Louis, drenched, tired, and hungry, Sarah rolled up to a café in front of which stood two dubious-looking characters. They had watched as her scarlet rain jacket—a striking complement to the lush rolling fields—bobbed up and down the hills like a float on a fishing line, in and out of view, for several miles before reaching them. "*Touriste!*" the men bantered with a glance toward each other. "So, how's the horse?" one of them asked Sarah in his thick accent, hardly able to contain his amusement.

They followed her inside the café, where her naive, bubbly enthusiasm betrayed her American heritage. They entertained themselves by eavesdropping on her conversation with an older couple who had just attended a funeral for a dear friend. "Where are you from? What's your work? Why are you in France? How long will you stay?" they asked, bombarding her.

That evening, at Lisa Michelle's *chambre d'hôte*, the rented room where Sarah would be living for the next four months, she discovered that one of the men who had teased her was himself an American. *The nerve!* she fumed to herself. *What does he have to go on about?*

Pascal, the real Breton of the two, remembers how Sarah stormed over to their lobster boat the following day; shuffled about, berating the pompous American for his patronizing behavior; and stomped off again. "Rather charming, really," Pascal says of her display.

The three ended up at the café that evening, and Sarah had her first conversation with Pascal. Like many tourists, she'd come to the west coast of Brittany with the preconceived notion that the country people there were uneducated and knew very little of the outside world, that it was a hermetically sealed microcosm of Celtic culture. But why was this man, Pascal, so well versed in Latin American history and politics? With surprise and pleasure she let go of her prejudice.

The next morning, when Pascal turned up at Madame Michelle's door, Sarah eagerly accepted his invitation to venture out with him on his lobster boat, a traditional Breton craft, and take photographs—if it ever stopped raining. Then, after a hurried "Be at the pier in fifteen minutes," he drove off in his van, leaving a bewildered Sarah to get thoroughly drenched as she rode her bike to meet him. "A passing shower," Pascal now says in his melodic voice. "One doesn't want to be seen as doing too much, at least not at first," he adds with a twinkle in his eye.

Their next date was a megalithic tour. "All I remember was following his back through the muck and sediment that bolstered the standing stones," laughs Sarah. "I could hardly keep up with him, he was moving so fast."

"He's a rogue!" Madame Michelle said comfortingly when Sarah recounted the experience of that afternoon.

Yet Sarah found herself undeniably attracted to Pascal—even with his abrupt and less-than-chivalrous behavior. So when he invited her out for dinner the following week, she tried her best to spiff up her scant wardrobe. In a small village, news—and gossip—travels fast. The curiosity of the village women brought out their generous natures, and soon one after another was knocking on Madame Michelle's door with a piece of polyester clothing or a pair of shoes ("about four sizes too small") for Sarah to try on. She remembers: "I pieced myself together with a borrowed skirt, my black high-top tennis shoes, a purple head scarf, and my red jacket."

This time Pascal actually *drove* Sarah to the restaurant, but when they pulled up in front he jumped out of the van and, without saying a word, grabbed a bucket of lobsters and tramped through the front door. When Sarah didn't follow, he went out and beckoned to her. He wasn't just delivering the lobsters, as she had thought; he was *bartering* them for their dinner.

"That's when the romance really began for me," says Sarah. "He disarmed me with his entertaining sense of humor and winsome storytelling. All the charm he'd been hiding came flooding out that night. The dinner and his company were fantastic."

Six months later Pascal followed Sarah to the east coast (of North America). And after thirteen years they continue to spend their summers in Brittany, where Sarah has photographed many of the inhabitants.

ε☙ Cupid says:

> After you have been in a relationship with someone for a while, it's easy to look back and recognize that when you met that person, you needed something that only she or he could provide—even though you might not have been conscious of what it was at the time. Usually people look for a widening of experience, personal acceptance, and enjoyment in the company of the other person. When you find all three, there's a match.

~ 39 ~

# Stage-Door Johnny

It was during summer stock at the Hilltop Theater in Baltimore that Joy was playing the lead in *Mr. and Mrs. North*. The navy was in town, and two sailors had come to that evening's performance. One of the sailors especially wanted to meet Joy and asked the stage manager to introduce them so he could take her out to dinner.

Howard Hughes's agent was also in the audience, ready to take Joy out for drinks and a possible movie contract. A serious actress, Joy had no trouble deciding which invitation to accept; she drew a mustache on her face with greasepaint before she went to meet the sailors and decline their invitation.

Not to be deterred, the naval ensign, Bob, returned the next evening with flowers and a good friend who, coincidentally, had grown up in Massachusetts with Joy. They all had a rollicking evening. Every night, with flowers in his arms, the sailor returned until his ship, the U.S.S. *Charles Carroll*, sailed for North Africa. He knew she was the woman for him.

Six months later he was back on American soil, asking for Joy's hand in marriage. "That was *fifty* years ago," says Joy incredulously. "Now young people tell me, 'Six months?' They wouldn't dream of marrying someone after such a brief time. But I've never regretted it."

᏶᠍᠍᠍ Cupid says:

> Don't be a Johnny- or a Jill-come-lately. Send those yellow roses or red tulips or magenta gladiolus to the one you love today. And remember: persistence pays off. Used within reason, your determination is your biggest ally and will help persuade and convince a wavering heart.

# Self-Defense

For two months that fall Kalen had been taking an afternoon aikido class. In mid-November there was an evening demonstration of new aikido moves by several black belts. "The voice of the announcer gave me chills," remembers Kalen. "It was so strong and sexy." But in the crowded room she couldn't see the face of the man behind the voice.

An ankle injury incurred that night prevented Kalen from attending classes for the next six weeks. When she returned, fully committed to doing her best, she had a new instructor—the sexy voice from the previous month's demonstration. Dan now remembers, "I was ready to meet a woman and get married; I was definitely looking for my mate. I was attracted by her beautiful curly hair and her tight jeans."

"I can't say it was love at first sight," says Kalen, "but a little voice inside suggested, 'This man will be an important person in your life.'"

Kalen's daughter, Melissa, was six years old at the time. Since her relationship with Melissa was of primary importance to Kalen, she paid careful attention to how the men she met interacted with her daughter. During the Christmas holiday season Kalen brought Melissa to aikido practice with her. "Dan did everything right. He was caring and attentive to Melissa, which helped to win my heart," Kalen says.

In addition to being a place for strengthening one's physical and spiritual discipline, the aikido dojo was also a social focus for many of its members. Every year it sponsored a gala New Year's Eve party and potluck. During the course of the party, as Dan became more relaxed, the clown in him announced over the microphone that whoever guessed the secret ingredient in Kalen's delicious dip would get to kiss her. This updated version of spin-the-bottle was news to Kalen, but she didn't mind at all when Dan correctly shouted out, "Artichokes!" and stood before her to collect the reward he himself had established.

"We were the last people to leave," sighs Kalen.

"It had been a perfect evening," agrees Dan.

It was also Kalen's twenty-ninth birthday. One year later to the day, Dan asked Kalen to marry him.

꧁ Cupid says:

> Timing is one of the most important variables in the dating game. You may think you're ready to make that total commitment, but if the person to whom you are attracted is

married or just leaving a relationship or is more interested in establishing a professional career—alone—you may be at a loss. A couple's coming together requires availability and willingness on both sides.

~ 41 ~

# The Bare Facts

It was a Unitarian family summer camp, much like any other family summer camp—except that it allowed nudity. Samantha had been enjoying vacations at the camp for three years when she met George. He noticed her first: the tall, full-bodied, redheaded beauty who loved to swim and really seemed to know how to have a good time.

They were both middle-aged and divorced, with grown children. He was a dentist; she catered. After a number of disappointing love affairs, Samantha had given up on the possibility of meeting her match and had settled into a productive and contented life that revolved around work and friends.

George waited until dinner that night to make his move. "There was something special about her," he recalls. "I knew this could be important, so I wanted to do everything right. I didn't want to make her uncomfortable by approaching her while we were naked." It turned out that Samantha had also noticed George and felt the same way, but hoped he would initiate their meeting.

When that evening's dessert was set out on trays so that the diners could serve themselves, George quickly grabbed two bowls and headed for the empty chair next to Samantha.

He had gone over their imagined dialogue in his mind several times during the day:

*Hi, I'm George and I couldn't help noticing you at the pool today.* No, that would make her too self-conscious.

*Don't I know you?* No, anyone could see through that line!

*Is this your first time at Camp Willoughby?* No, he had to say something funny, something original.

"Do you always vacation at nudist camps?" he smiled, handing her a serving of cherry cobbler. "Only during warm weather," she laughed, meeting his warm brown eyes with anticipation.

They spent the rest of the evening, and well into the next morning, bundled up around a blazing bonfire, getting the particulars about the person each felt he or she had always known.

George and Samantha still enjoy warm-weather vacations at the camp, but now they go as a married couple.

### ஃ Cupid says:

Only half of beauty is in the eye of the beholder; we carry the other half in our image of ourselves. Feeling good about who you are and confident about how you look is *real* sex appeal. It has less to do with the clothes or makeup you wear than with how you carry yourself. Don't be coerced by the media and the advertising industry into hating your body because you don't look like the models in TV ads or women's and men's magazines. Remember, it's easy to air-brush away so-called imperfections on a photograph, but character is what makes you unique, what makes you laugh and cry and love.

# 42

# The Campaign Workers

It was a victory party for a local political candidate. Both Jules and Shirley had been volunteers on the campaign. Shirley had noticed Jules, a handsome, white-bearded man in his late sixties, among the hundred or so party attendees, but he had seemed "so formidable, so stern in that German sort of way." Anyway, there was too much smoke, loud music, and rich food for her taste that night. So she went into the kitchen and, thanking the hostess, bade her an early good night.

Overhearing the conversation, Jules invited Shirley to sit out on the veranda for a while and talk. Shirley, just fifty, had heard from a few of her women friends about Jules's reputation with women. "He loves women and dates everyone he finds attractive who will go out with him," one friend had told her. So she wasn't at all surprised when he offered to follow her home and keep her company. She was game.

After a bottle of wine in front of a cozy fire, she found Jules irresistible, and the two "hit the sack," as Shirley describes it, within an hour. "I woke up in the morning and knew that this was the rest of my life. My only regret is that it took me until I was fifty to really fall in love." They have now been married for twelve years.

### ৡ Cupid says:

People behave differently with different people. Give each person you meet a fresh chance, even though you may have heard unfavorable gossip about him. Find out for yourself who she is rather than adopt the bias of another, since you do not know that person's motives. Jealousy? Revenge? Dissatisfaction? Simple confusion? Take responsibility for getting to know someone on your own and relish the pleasure of learning through your own insight, resources, and experiences.

# 43

# How Much Is That Painting in the Window?

Sometime in 1941 before the United States entered World War II, Page Smith was on maneuvers with the Twenty-ninth Infantry Division in Charlotte, North Carolina. Walking through town with his buddies, he came across a window exhibition of watercolors at the local Sherwin-Williams paint store. Page was taken by their sophisticated similarity to John Marin's work.

During the following week he thought often of the paintings. When he returned the next Saturday to purchase one, the exhibition had been removed. However, the store clerk was helpful in locating the artist for Page.

A heavily accented southern voice answered his inquiring telephone call. The voice belonged to Eloise, a nineteen-year-old student at Charlotte's all-female Queen's College.

Once they had met, Page was completely captivated by the young, spunky blonde who had won first place at the Young Americans Exhibition at the Whitney Museum in New York City the previous year. "My immediate reaction was, 'She's much too beautiful for me!'" he says. But he bravely asked for a date and she accepted.

"Times were different then," Eloise says. "You didn't jump into bed with anyone, the way people do these days."

On the second date Page asked if he could kiss Eloise. On the third date he made a quantum leap and asked her to marry him. They have lived a charmed life since then—and she'd never even heard of John Marin.

### ⅌ Cupid says:

The soul of an artist or writer shines through in his or her work. Be willing to extend yourself in friendship to those whose artistry you admire. In 1925 Robert Graves, the poet and novelist best known for his historical novel *I, Claudius*, read a poem by an American woman named Laura Riding and knew they were destined to be together. After he contacted her and told her of his "discovery," she sailed for Europe to meet him. They became involved and, a few years later, settled on the island of Majorca, where they lived for ten years.

There are countless hidden pleasures to be found in the arts, not the least of which is the pure enjoyment of them. Take an art history class or a poetry appreciation course. Join the local opera club or start a reading group.

~ 44 ~

# Kibitzing in Israel

Ariella, an Israeli, and her first husband had gone to a kibbutz in the hope of saving their marriage. Aaron, who was a dual citizen of the United States and Israel, had been drafted into the Israeli Army. Having lived on a kibbutz ten years earlier, he requested that the kibbutz "adopt" him during his enlistment. That meant that he would be allowed to return every two to three weeks on an eighteen-hour leave for rest and recuperation.

Their meeting became inevitable, especially after Aaron broke his leg during maneuvers and was stationed at the kibbutz during his recovery. For Aaron, the attraction was immediate. He was smitten by Ariella's North African beauty, her green eyes that were "like quartz crystals, always changing colors." For Ariella, it was more of a flirtation—which is where they kept it until her marriage soon dissolved completely.

One day, Ariella invited Aaron to go swimming with her and the children from the day-care center where she worked. "I saw how much fun he was and recognized the spark between us," she says. They became inseparable. After Aaron's leg healed, though, he had to go back to the barracks during the week, returning to the kibbutz on weekends.

The following year, his tour of duty completed, Aaron was accepted into the doctoral program of the Department of Geography at the University of Wisconsin. The next problem: how to take Ariella with him. After several trips to Tel Aviv trying to work out a solution, it seemed to them, though they were a bit reluctant, that marriage was the only answer. They bought a four-day junket to Cyprus, the closest city that would perform a civil ceremony. Aaron rationalizes their deferment of a religious ceremony by saying, "You can fib to the Immigration and Naturalization Service, but not to God." Four days later, they returned to Israel as husband and wife.

It wasn't exactly a shotgun wedding, but Aaron realized after they had set up a home in Wisconsin together that their relationship was, in his words, "a fait accompli." He adds, "The male in me got scared." It was during a return visit to Israel, in fact, some months later that the romantic in Aaron triumphed. Ariella remembers the moonlit waters at Hertzelia Beach and how he proposed to her on one knee. "He consciously chose me," she says. "I already had my green card!" Eventually they were married in a religious ceremony.

"Yes, we were the original *Green Card* story," Aaron laughs, "several years before the film!"

## 🕊 Cupid says:

A communal settlement where people are allowed to come and live for an extended period of time is an optimal place for like-minded people to meet. Ethical and ideological values—and sometimes religious values as well—are important parts of you that you can share honestly with another. Both people don't necessarily have to have the same values, but their differences must be respected—and appreciated.

## ~ 45 ~

# All the World's a Stage

"I thought Texas was a state you drove *around* so you didn't have to drive through," Lois jokes. Dixie was a Texan steak-and-potatoes kind of gal, and Lois was a strict vegetarian. It was at the auditions for *Amazon All-Stars*, by Carolyn Gage, that Lois first laid eyes on Dixie. "She sparkled. The whole stage lit up when she stood on it," Lois remembers. Because Lois was in a committed ten-year relationship, she tried earnestly to deny her immediate attraction toward Dixie.

As fate would have it, they were both cast in the play. Lois's role was as the indecisive pitcher and manager of a women's softball team. Dixie was a shortstop who was good at stealing bases—a metaphor for stealing hearts.

"Dixie's role as a promiscuous heartbreaker in the play had me confused with who she was in real life," admits Lois. "In fact, one day, feeling very self-righteous, I said to her, 'You're not going to be happy until you sleep with everyone in this play, are you?'" Staying in character and with her best Texas accent, Dixie drawled, "No, *ma'am.*"

Torn between her budding romantic interest in Dixie and her loyalty to her existing relationship, Lois tried her best to stay clear of Dixie, but they kept getting paired up during warm-up practices. One day during a dance rehearsal, the director instructed the cast to form a circle and told those who would naturally be the initiator to hang back, and those who would usually be waiting to be asked to dance to be the instigator. Since both Dixie and Lois were normally initiators, they both waited to be approached. They waited until they were the only two left standing in the circle.

"Looks like we're pardners, ma'am," Dixie smiled at Lois. Silently pleased, Lois couldn't get over how beautifully they danced together. "I knew I was in trouble!" she says.

After that evening, Lois would look forward with genuine longing to seeing Dixie at each performance. They began to spend more time together backstage, and Lois was slowly able to distinguish between the slutty *role* Dixie was playing and Dixie herself. Though she realized she was falling in love, Lois still sent mixed messages, alternating seductiveness with indifference: "I couldn't believe that I was falling in love with a woman who drove a truck and talked about having a shotgun!" Neither had been willing to admit to the other, or to herself, that there was anything but a casual flirtation going on between them.

One day Lois took the initiative and suggested that they meet at the beach. As they sat side by side on a rock trying to keep their feet dry, their cheeks briefly brushed against each other. Lois says she was "flooded with love," that she "felt a new kind of sensual awakening."

Even though Lois immediately told her partner about the new development, both Dixie and Lois agreed to keep the news of their love from the rest of the cast. "In the play, we weren't even supposed to *like* each other, and now we'd gone and fallen in love," laughs Dixie. "I'm sure they knew more than they let on." During a scene in which they had to make up a bed, they could hardly contain their excitement at knowing that eventually they would be making their own bed together.

The hardest part for Lois was trusting her feelings, trusting love: "I realized that true strength is in giving your heart. I'd been hurt so many times, my heart was crusty." Like many people, she tried to hide behind her prejudices: "I had to examine why I wanted Dixie to be different than she was—which was wonderful. Why did I want her to be like me instead of herself?" Once she was able to relinquish trying to have control over the relationship, she eased into what she describes as "the best one I've ever had." And they continue to make their bed together.

## ❧ Cupid says:

The lesson for Lois was to let go of her prejudices and her desire to control the feelings and actions of another. Why is it that when you meet and fall in love with someone, the first thing you try to do is change that person? A human being is a complete system of complexity: family history, personal development and experiences, likes and dislikes, dreams and fears. No one is perfect. And within those very qualities that may keep you from perfection you find your uniqueness and individuality, your attractiveness, your humanity. You already live in a society that promotes conformity; don't cultivate it in yourself and your mate.

## ～ 46 ～

# Incarcerated Love

What he missed most on the inside was the love of a good woman. Jim was doing time in the state penitentiary and spent his days working out with weights, baking in the prison kitchen, drawing surreal images on paper, and writing and playing music. Sandy was the director of the arts program at the prison.

Sandy found some of the men gorgeous, but they were off limits to the staff. When Jim became Sandy's personal assistant, the sparks began to fly. A friend jokingly had told Sandy, "A convict makes a great husband: you always know where he is, he thinks about you constantly, he's always glad to see you, he writes to you every day, you have incredible sex once a month, and you have lots of free time."

After a year of hiding their love, Jim and Sandy were married within the prison walls. Even though he had ten more years to serve, the marriage at least allowed them the benefit of conjugal visits and gave Jim a home to look forward to after his release.

### ৯৯ Cupid says:

You never know where or when you are going to meet someone who is interesting to you and could contribute to your growth and happiness. Don't be afraid to volunteer at your local hospital, retirement home, homeless shelter, animal shelter, or school district. Deep satisfaction is derived from giving of yourself, and the practice of giving opens your heart to unexpected people and events.

## ~ 47 ~

# The Doctor with a Heart

For sixteen years he'd been her family physician, and Barbara had always joked about how much she loved her doctor, how caring and understanding he was.

It wasn't until Rich joined the performing choir, of which Barbara was already a member, that they had a chance to begin to know something about each other's personal lives. They discovered that they both were enduring unhappy, nearly intolerable marriages.

Respectful of the complex situation, they remained supportive friends and didn't ask of one another what they themselves could not give. But life has its own twists and turns.

Eventually, they each separated from their respective spouses and began to see the possibility of love between them. "We very definitely had developed a solid friendship based on caring, trust, and communication," Barbara says. "When we were finally able to untangle our individual lives, we each had our best friend waiting for us."

ᓭ Cupid says:

Sometimes a person you've known for a long time and with whom you are very comfortable suddenly takes on a romantic aura and you realize she or he may be best suited to be your mate. Remember that physical attraction may wane, but the communication skills you take the time to develop will cement your friendship and are likely to endure.

~ 48 ~

# Soul Mates

Linda met Keith during a trip to Bali to study the Balinese healing arts with a group of Jungian-oriented professionals.

Keith noticed Linda first at the group's initial itinerary-planning meeting in California and was instantly tantalized by the woman with the unique appearance. *Is she Native American, Italian, Hispanic?* he wondered to himself. She was charismatic yet very natural. She had a vulnerability that couldn't quite hide a distinct brilliance. They didn't speak that night, but her presence stayed with him.

On the flight, Linda sat one row behind him, engrossed in a book of poetry. It seemed as if she barely noticed him. During a three-day layover in Australia the two began to converse. She saw in Keith a sensitive, thoughtful, vigorous, and vital man of fifty-eight. She was excited by his spirit of adventure and athletic ability. But it was on the day he brought two roses—one for Linda and one for the oldest woman on the tour—that she also saw an irresistible romantic.

The evening they arrived in Bali the group was greeted by a sultry sea breeze and a sunset painted in regal purple, mauve, and turquoise. Bali was magical. It was sensual. It was romantic.

Linda and Keith walked together that night under the stars and along the beach, following a gently lapping current. They spent their first night together, and remained inseparable during their three-week stay. When the other members of the tour group voted to move to a newer, more westernized hotel, Keith and Linda savored the good fortune of their privacy in the humble native bungalows with verandas and views that looked out to distant verdant mountains and lush, terraced rice paddies.

Linda's first book, called *The Wounded Woman*, had just been published. Although it was destined to become a best-seller, no one had yet read or even heard of it. Once he'd learned about the book, Keith was eager to read it and get a fuller perspective on this woman with whom he was quickly falling in love.

They soon realized they each had met their equal in the other. "Linda was a very passionate woman who not only loved the opera and theater, poetry and nature, but was able to grasp the mystical presence of the Divine within them as well," says Keith. "We had a fiery connection!"

What ultimately won Linda's heart was the recognition that Keith was on a similar spiritual journey: "One of the major attractions between us was that we were both connected to the mystical and the wilderness. I found my soul mate."

Keith responded to Linda's book in a deep way. He was supportive of her creative process in a manner that was new to them both. He alternately encouraged her work and challenged her to push herself further. They seemed a perfect match and spent their time hiking, going to temples, and attending rituals and ceremonies.

When the three-week study tour came to a close, they looked forward to returning to the San Francisco Bay area, where they both lived, and continuing their life journey together—which is what they have done for the past twelve years. Two years after their meeting, Linda was inspired to write about what she calls "the soul mate journey" in her second book, *On the Way to the Wedding*.

### ࿔ Cupid says:

Linda and Keith were on a spiritual quest. Whether your interest is in scholarly research of the Dead Sea Scrolls in Israel, in embracing your Celtic roots in Ireland, or in something as quotidian as attending a ceremony, lecture, or group discussion at the religious center of your choice, a connection to the mystical is the outcome of one's individual spiritual pursuit. So go out in pursuit of the spiritual. Even if you don't meet your soul mate, you will encounter your soul.

~ 49 ~

# Twice in a Lifetime

The place was Saint Bede's Catholic Church in Williamsburg, Virginia; the date was April 12, 1989. *How could so many years have slipped by so quickly?* Mel thought to himself as he stood at the same altar, beside the same best man, as he had forty-two years earlier when he and Polly, his college sweetheart, had married. They had been married for nearly forty years before she died of cancer.

Carrying on with his life as a bachelor, Mel continued to travel internationally with the Saint Mary's College rugby team as a mentor, to visit his eight children dotted throughout the United States and England, and to oversee his regional real-estate investments in central California. Mel had never believed in miracles; he believed in hard work and commitment. That had been proven when he won his way out of the small Pennsylvania mining town on a football scholarship to William and Mary College, and again when he flew a bomber over Germany during the Second World War, and again when he did his best to support—financially, emotionally, and spiritually—his family of ten.

Mel had loved living on the East Coast, and his football years had been among the best in his life. That's why he looked forward to college reunions in general, but especially to the one coming up—the first-ever reunion of football players, coaches, and cheerleaders. How could he know that this weekend would change his life?

~ ~ ~

Carol was a vibrant, youthful woman in her sixties who, even though she'd been mourning the loss of her husband, Warren, for the past year, still carried the spunk and enthusiasm of her cheerleading days at William and Mary. At the behest of her sister and brother-in-law, she agreed to attend the college athletic reunion, which she would never have done on her own. It would be fun, she thought, and so good to see old friends again.

It turned out that Carol's brother-in-law, Jack, was one of Mel's close college chums. Carol and Mel met that night through Jack. They hadn't known each other in college, and the flush of emotional excitement they both felt on their initial meeting contrasted with the image they had of themselves as widow and widower. Still, just for that evening, they enjoyed each other's company.

"I was pleased to meet you last weekend . . ." Thus Mel cautiously began his letter to Carol as he flew back to California. How could he respectfully express his interest, he wondered, without sounding presumptuous? And what *was* his interest? He decided to remain circumspect. When the plane landed he mailed the letter to Carol's Virginia address, and waited. After hearing nothing for two weeks, he took her silence for her answer.

≈ ≈ ≈

"Mary, remember the man at the reunion I told you about?" Carol asked her daughter several weeks later. "When I returned home from my trip to New York a letter from him was waiting for me. Read this. What do you suppose he's trying to tell me?"

"That he wants to *see* you again, Mother!" Mary replied with the subtle undertone of *Don't you get it?* that only a parent can hear.

"What should I do?"

"Call him, immediately. Let him know you're open."

≈ ≈ ≈

One year later, the whole thing smacked of the miraculous to Mel. Here he stood, the same groom in the same church in the same town, with the same best man. But the bride was different. The seasons were different, too. Before, the wedding had been in November—going into winter; now they were just coming out of it.

### ஜ Cupid says:

Sharing a common history is an important link for people who are looking for a mate. There is nothing like mutual experience to develop a bond. High-school and college reunions are natural meeting places, as are extended gatherings of family and friends and work-related reunions. Often, after the loss of a beloved mate, people think their romantic lives are over. Yet for many, such as Carol and Mel, a new life is just waiting to begin. Miracles do happen.

# The Jazz Singer

It was love at first sight for Monty. There she stood onstage right before him—Kitty, the luscious red-haired vocalist with the throaty laugh. The San Francisco jazz club was crowded that night. Kitty had been steadily building a sizable following. The legendary singer Jon Hendricks had even written the liner notes for her newly released CD, *Evolution*, Monty noticed as he read the notes.

Kitty crooned and caressed some old standards, imbuing them with her inimitable neo-bebop style. When she belted out "Please Send Me Someone to Love," Monty felt she was singing only to him. Because he was sitting with a group of jazz producers interested in bringing Kitty to their private club, Monty had a guaranteed introduction. He was definitely smitten. As soon as he got home Monty looked up Kitty's telephone number. "You're *terrific!*" he told her answering machine, without leaving a return number.

Within a few weeks Monty went to see Kitty perform again. "There was obviously something happening besides music appreciation," he laughs. She invited him out for coffee at Mario's Bohemian Cigar Store, and they walked the streets of North Beach for hours reading restaurant menus and sharing their passionate interest in food and cooking. It turned out the two had a great deal more in common: Monty was a jazz musician himself; he played the saxophone and had recorded an album in London. They went up to Kitty's apartment, where he played his cassette for her, and the next thing they knew it was three in the morning and he was saying good-bye.

Monty knew she was soon leaving for a monthlong gig in Holland—the land of his birth, where his family still lived. "I'd like to see you once again before you go," he said the next morning on the telephone. During their date he convinced Kitty to visit his mother and grandmother, who still lived in the same house in which he was born in The Hague. *Why not?* she thought. *This is an experience I wouldn't normally have.*

"As soon as I arrived in Holland, Monty started calling and writing ten-page romantic letters which he'd Fed Ex so I would receive them the following day," she remembers. "For all he spent in telephone and postage fees he could have bought *two* plane tickets!"

"I have your picture in my lap while I'm writing to you," one letter read.

*Good. Go for my ego!* she laughed to herself.

"Monty's mother was very proper. I was so nervous," says Kitty. "There I was—I hardly knew Monty and I had no idea how his mother would respond to a female jazz singer." But they ended up having a lovely afternoon together. The clincher was discovering that mother and girlfriend had the same birthday: November 7. "It was funny, though, because she thought I knew Monty much better than I did. I mean, we'd only had *two* dates. She kept saying, 'Isn't it funny when Alfonso does such and such?' I thought, *Who's Alfonso?* It took me a while to realize that 'Alfonso' was Monty's given name."

Back in California, Monty was convinced that Kitty was the woman for him. "My grandmother was in her nineties, and I wanted Kitty to have a chance to meet her. As it turned out, it was extremely fortuitous because my grandmother died the following year and her house [which has since become a national landmark] was sold. I wanted Kitty to see my roots, and I also wanted my family to experience her."

One month later, when Kitty flew home, Monty was waiting for her with open arms. "He seemed so sincere. I thought, *So, he's guileless. It's not the worst thing a person can be.*"

Four and a half years later they were married, and now Monty beams when Kitty sings "Please Send Me Someone to Love."

## ଛଢ Cupid says:

People have lost the art of courtship and letter writing. The imposed separation Kitty and Monty experienced actually gave them the advantage of getting to know each other more slowly, through a written correspondence, without the pressure that physical presence induces. Writing letters broadened the romantic aspect of their courtship. And, when you meet and fall in love with someone, it's wise to remember that his or her family is also part of the package.

*Cathleen Rountree and her beloved Sienna.*

If you would like to see your story in
*50* More *Ways to Meet Your Lover,*
please send your experiences (along with
a stamped, self-addressed envelope) to:

Cathleen Rountree
50 Ways
P.O. Box 552
Aptos, CA 95001